the art of HELPING IV

Robert R. Carkhuff, Ph. D.
with
Richard M. Pierce, Ph. D. and John R. Cannon, Ph. D.

CARKHUFF
INSTITUTE
of HUMAN
TECHNOLOGY

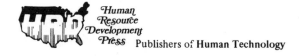

Human
Resource
Development
Press   Publishers of Human Technology

Copyright © 1980 by
Human Resource Development Press, Inc.
22 Amherst Rd., Dept. M10, Amherst, Massachusetts 01002
413-253-3488

Fourth Edition

First Printing, January 1980
Second Printing, January 1981
Third Printing, January 1982
Fourth Printing, January 1983

Library of Congress Catalog Card No. 79-91075
International Standard Book No. 0-914234-10-2

Designed and Illustrated by Tom Capolongo
Indexed by Bob and Kate Harris
Typeset by Sims Enterprises, Abington, MA
Paste-up by Dave Coburn and Jim Burke
Printed and Bound by Progressive Packaging
  and Printing, Milton Village, MA

the art of HELPING IV

I

PREFACE

The first edition of **The Art of Helping** in 1972 represented an attempt to distill helping theory and research into simple and useful helping skills. Four editions, and nearly 200,000 readers later, we are still working to improve **The Art of Helping** to better meet its users' needs.

Each edition has spawned new empirical inquiries resulting in further refinements. As a result, the basic model and the skills incorporated within **Helping IV** are the most thoroughly researched helping tools in the history of counseling and psychotherapy. Each edition has been shaped by the professors, trainers and helpers who have used it. Thus **Helping IV** stands as our best attempt to identify and teach the skills that effective helpers have found to be useful.

Those of you familiar with previous editions will find the same, simple, step-by-step presentation of concrete skills you found so effective and easy to teach. The Fourth Edition is still designed to be used in inservice helper training and college courses from Junior College through Graduate School. Counselors, social workers, health care practitioners, teachers, employers and parents will find these skills useful. Wherever courses or training programs place a priority on skill development, the Fourth Edition will be useful.

The changes in this edition increase its usefulness as a teaching tool. A summary of carefully selected research literature has been added to give a clear and simple picture of the vast empirical base supporting these skills. A set of discussion questions has been added to the beginning of each chapter to help readers begin the chapter with an awareness of their personal experiences with each skill. A new, more concrete scale for discriminating helping behaviors will aid in assessing effective helping. Many of the skills have been refined by including more explicit questions that highly-skilled helpers mentally answer while engaged in helping someone. An expanded feeling word vocabulary will make it easier for readers to increase their repertoires of feeling words. An author and subject index has been added to facilitate easy access to the information in **Helping IV**.

To make the text more useful, a Student Workbook has been developed. This workbook will help the reader bridge the gap between reading about the skills in **Helping IV** and practicing them in a training session. Additional teaching tools are currently being developed.

Just as this text has grown and changed, so do we as teachers, trainers and helpers need to grow and change.

If we do not live and die growing, then it is as if we were never here at all — for ourselves and others.

January 1980

R.R.C.
R.M.P.
J.R.C.

ABOUT THE AUTHORS

Dr. Robert R. Carkhuff is Chairman, Board of Directors, Carkhuff Institute of Human Technology (C.I.H.T.). The author of more than two dozen books, he is the most-cited author in counseling literature, and one of the 100 most-cited social scientists of our time.

Dr. John R. Cannon is Director of Management Systems, C.I.H.T. A lifelong counselor and administrator, he is also co-author of **The Skills of Helping** and **The Psychiatric Rehabilitation Practice Series.**

Dr. Richard M. Pierce is Director of Human Technology, C.I.H.T. An experienced counselor and educator, he is co-author of **Helping Begins at Home** and **The Skills of Teaching.**

1

introduction

Have you ever experienced different families in their natural habitats? Have you ever noticed how dramatically differently they function?

One family is so vital. Its members are so involved in their personal interests. Talking about what they are talking about. Yet responsive to each other's needs. This is the facilitative family.

The other is so painful. Its members are trapped within their own experience. Never talking about what they are talking about. And so oblivious to each other's needs. This is the retarding family.

What do you think happens to the various members of the two different families over time? If you study the people over a period of time, you will see dramatically different effects.

The members of the facilitative family are in the process of becoming persons. The members of the retarding family are becoming non-persons.

Facilitators and Retarders

In the facilitative family, the more mature members have an expanding wholeness that incorporates the welfare of their various family members. While they have developed their creative initiatives in their learning and working arenas, they are responsive to the experience of the immature family members. Indeed, they serve as models and agents for the development of others' creative initiatives.

All members are developing and integrating their physical, emotional and intellectual resources in such a manner as to have skillful applications available to them in their daily existence. However much any one member may slip — physically, emotionally or intellectually — the deterioration is only temporary. To be sure, the facilitative family treats each crisis as an opportunity for the further growth and development of its members.

The mature members of the facilitative family transmit their vitality to the immature in an ongoing attempt to energize the actualizing process for the latter. Ultimately, they recognize their essential interdependency and become one with their worlds. In so doing, they incorporate their own humanity.

Growing

In the retarding family, none of the members are mature in the sense of seeing beyond themselves. They are caught up inside of their own skins as they strive for a pseudo-independence from their worlds. Their careers are characterized by creative imitativeness rather than initiative: they dedicate themselves only to "looking good" with over-achieving B's, "making the team", and guarding their bureaucratic jobs once they have seized them; their specialty is developing more "practical" and "political" variations of the products of the innovators.

While they may have the apparency of child-centeredness, the chronological adults in these families have not the energy, nor the disposition, nor the response repertoire, to follow through on such a bold program. They are never there when needed because they are physically ill, emotionally exhausted or intellectually stale. They are always there when not needed: hovering at readiness to embrace like a drowning swimmer in a death dive.

You can only depend upon their instability. Perhaps it is better that way, for to become intensely involved with them is to intimately know deterioration.

Deteriorating

Human relationships may have facilitative or retarding effects. Like a marriage, the consequences of all human relationships may be "for better" or "for worse." The consequences for one or more of the people involved may be constructive or destructive.

This basic research finding holds for all relationships. Like the facilitative and retarding families, the relationships are producing persons and non-persons. Whether teacher-student or counselor-counselee or health care provider-patient or employer-employee relationships, the effects may be positive or negative or any of the degrees in between these extremes.

The effects are seen in physical, emotional and intellectual functioning. With facilitative agents, the recipients may be physically energetic, emotionally expansive and intellectually acute. With retarding agents, the recipients may be physically listless, emotionally shallow and intellectually dull.

For Better or Worse

The effects of human relationships depend upon the power relationship. Like a marriage or a family, the effects depend upon who has the power in the relationship.

If the person who is ceded the power in the relationship is functioning at a high level, then all parties involved can benefit from the relationship. For example, if the parents are functioning at high levels — physically, emotionally and intellectually — then they can be models and agents of their children's growth and development.

Unfortunately, power relations are developed for reasons other than functionality — reasons like tradition, economics and politics. Consequently, if the person who is ceded the power is functioning at low levels, then all parties involved will deteriorate from the relationship. For example, if one or more of the parents are functioning at low levels of resource development, then they will be retarders of their children's growth and development. It makes good sense that if people have not discovered themselves, they can only handicap others in finding their own way in life.

Power Relationships

The effects of the power relationships depend upon skills. Most fundamentally, it is the powerful person's level of functioning in basic human relations skills that determines the effects of the relationships. There are two essential sets of skills which are the basic ingredients of all human relationships in all areas of human endeavor: responding skills and initiating skills.

In reality, these skills are cycled in an individual's personal development before his or her interpersonal development. That is, a person must respond to understand himself or herself before initiating an action program or product. Similarly, in interpersonal relationships, a person must respond to the experience of others before initiating action courses.

To be sure, you cannot respond fully if you have not initiated fully. There is no real understanding without acting upon that understanding. In the same manner, you cannot initiate fully if you have not responded fully. There is no effective action that is not based upon a depth of understanding.

We need to talk.

Skills Levels

Responsiveness is the basic ingredient of human relations. It involves empathy or seeing the world through another's eyes. It involves standing in another's place and experiencing the world the way s/he does. But responsiveness is more!

Responsiveness is the most profound variable in the human condition. To get outside of our own skins and to enter another and return, not only intact but phenomenologically larger; that is the test of empathy. To know more than that person does of her own experience, to be able to describe and predict and influence that experience constructively; that is the test of responsive skills.

Responsive skills, then, involve experiencing another's condition and communicating to her your experience. Further, responsive skills involve the other person in a process leading to her own self-exploration and self-understanding.

You've been worrying about this.

Responding Skills

Initiative is the basic ingredient of human functionality. Initiative involves seeing a goal and going after it. It involves operationalizing the goal or breaking it down into its components. It involves developing the steps and systems to achieve the goal. Yet initiative is more than a mechanical process.

Initiative begins with a vision of the possible. It involves throwing out a sky hook, often to a place where we have never been except in our fantasies as, for example, when as a nation, we put a person on the moon. It literally and physically involves pulling ourselves up by our own bootstraps.

Initiative skills, then, involve building upon our own experience to see a goal. Further, initiative skills stimulate the other person to take action to achieve the goal.

We'll have to make some sacrifices.

Initiating Skills

Before we go any further, let us stop to consider what your skills in helping are. When people share their problems with you, what skills do you have to truly show that you are responding to their experience? How do you physically show this? Emotionally? Intellectually?

What do you do and say that will reassure the people that you are sensitively attuned to their experience? How do you show you heard them? What feedback do you give?

When you are wrestling with their problems, how do you share your experience to help them to develop achievable goals that solve their problems? Now that you have responded to their experience, how do you help them to initiate steps to get to their goals?

Perhaps upon consideration you will realize that there are already a number of things that you do that are potentially helpful to people. Certainly, your intentions are to help them. Whether your good intentions will be translated into their personal benefits will depend, in the end, upon the helping skills you have to implement your intentions.

Taking Stock

Potentially, all relationships are helping relationships. It depends upon the helping skills you have. And the effects of the skills depend upon how you sequence them. Helping is, in a very real sense, a developmental process like child rearing. Effective parents initially respond to their children to insure that their basic needs are met. They give their children a feeling of security in an environment that might otherwise overwhelm them.

Effective parents also initiate or share with their children their learnings about life. These initiatives will help to facilitate the children's learnings. These initiatives will also help to guide the children's development by teaching them what was found to be effective.

Effective parenting involves both responsive and initiative skills. The parents respond to their children's experiences so that they can initiate effectively from their own. Indeed, this is the way that children learn to respond and initiate in their lives. The children model themselves after their parents, the learners after their teachers, the counselees after their counselors. Helpers who are fully responsive and fully initiative teach their helpees to be fully responsive and fully initiative.

Responsive and initiative behaviors are the basic dimensions of human development.

I want to be like you.

Developmental Model

AN OVERVIEW OF HELPING

Helping is a process leading to new behavior for the person being helped. An effective helper is initially nourishing or responsive. This nourishment prepares the person being helped for the more directionful or initiative behavior of the helper.

When the children are sufficiently nourished, they will involve themselves increasingly in the directionful activities of their parents. As they become capable of both nourishing and directionful behavior, they assume the mantle of adulthood and later, perhaps parenthood. They can act constructively in their own lives. They can act constructively in the lives of others. When the persons being helped can be fully nourishing and fully directionful, both in relation to themselves and others, we can say that they are fully adult. In other terms, we can say that **they are now helpers** for they are capable of helping others as well as themselves.

Persons who are fully alive help other persons to become fully alive.

Responsive and initiative behaviors are the basic dimensions of helping.

Helping

Before we can acquire the skills of helping, we must understand the goals of helping. We cannot help effectively if we do not understand where we are going. New behavior is the overall goal of helping.

In order for an individual to learn new behavior, she must first explore where she is. She simply cannot get to any goal if she does not first know where she is. She must explore herself in relation to herself. She must explore herself in relation to her world. We must know the problems before we can change the behavior.

I don't know
how I feel...

Exploring

In exploring herself, the person seeking help is attempting to **understand where she is in relation to where she wants to be.** The only purpose for exploration is understanding. In some way, someone has to help her to clarify her experience so that she may understand herself more deeply.

Now I know what
I need to do...

Understanding

Finally, self-understanding is not real until the individual has acted upon it. The only purpose for understanding behavior is to be able to act to learn new behavior. In acting, the person **acts upon how to get from where she is to where she wants to be.** The more accurately a person understands herself, the more constructively she can act—for herself and others.

My first
step is...

Acting

The process of exploration, understanding and action is one that recycles itself. When the client or helpee acts, she gets the feedback from her action. The feedback provides a stimulus to further self-exploration which, in turn, sets the stage for more accurate self-understanding. Real understanding, then, comes from the learning that follows action. Having calculated effective action, the helpee must now explore and understand the feedback which she gets. Finally, she modifies her action in accordance with a more accurate understanding of herself.

Exploration

Understanding

Action

Recycling

THE HELPER'S SKILLS IN HELPING

Most simply, the job of the helper is to provide assistance as the helpee explores where she is, understands where she is in relation to where she wants to be, and acts to get from where she is to where she wants to be.

I don't know what to do.

Helping Skills

Before the helper can facilitate helpee exploring, understanding and acting, she must involve the helpee in the
helping process. She does this by **attending** or giving her
attention to the helpee. Attending gives the helpee the feeling
of security that makes the helpee's involvement in the helping
process possible.

Attending Involving

In order to help the helpee explore where she is, the helper needs to **respond** to the helpee. The helper responds to the helpee by entering the helpee's frame of reference and communicating an understanding of the helpee's experience. Responding gives the helpee the *"I am with you"* feeling of freedom and encouragement that facilitates the helpee's exploration of her experience.

Responding Exploring

In order to help the helpee understand where she is in relation to where she wants to be, the helper needs to **personalize** the helpee's experience. Personalizing moves beyond simply responding to the helpee's experience and adds the helper's perspective on why the helpee's experience is so important to her and what her personal deficits are that are contributing to the problem. Based on this personalized understanding, the helpee is able to identify important goals in her life.

So your goal is
to share more of
your feelings with others.

Yeah, I really
want to be myself.

Personalizing Understanding

Finally, in order to help the helpee act to get from where she is to where she wants to be, the helper needs to **initiate** with the helpee.

Initiating involves developing a specific plan to reach the goal.

Together, by communicating fully, the helper and helpee develop all the steps that the helpee needs to take to act constructively in her world.

STEPS

1
2

Your next step is to find some ways to express those feelings.

My first step is to label my feelings.

Initiating ▶ Acting

The skills of helping lead directly to the goals of helping. Each helpee goal builds upon the last goal. Each helper skill builds upon the last skill.

Together these goals and skills provide a simple road map to guide you through the complex process of helping another human being. Whenever you get lost, simply go back to your road map...

Helper Skills: Attending ▶ Responding   Personalizing   Initiating

Helpee Goals: Exploration   Understanding   Action

The Helping Model

In the following pages, helping will be broken down into these four learning tasks: **attending; responding; personalizing; initiating.**

As you learn these basic tasks, you will periodically be assigned persons seeking help. They may be formal clients, students in your class, or other informal helpees. They may be friends, colleagues or associates. Or they may simply be the people you meet for five minutes at the bus stop.

What they all have in common is that they need help. Some may hurt very deeply. Some may be troubled by situations that can be changed readily. Others may simply be motivated to learn new behavior.

You will learn to help.

Learning to Help

HELPING SKILLS PRE-TEST

As a starting point in learning to help, you will probably want to assess your current level of helping skills. You will have an opportunity to check out both your ability to communicate helpfully and your ability to discriminate helpful responses.

Imagine that you have been interacting with the following helpee for about 30 minutes.

The helpee is a 19-year-old student who is having problems deciding what major to select at the end of her sophomore year in college. She says to you:

"I really don't know what to do. My parents have been pushing nursing for a long time and that's what I thought I wanted, too. But this term I've really gotten into a math course and I've been thinking about trying engineering. It's really confusing and nobody seems to be able to help me."

On the following lines, write out what you would say to this helpee. Try to communicate both understanding and direction. Write the exact words you would use if you were actually speaking to the helpee.

_____

_____

_____

_____

Communicating Helping Skills

It's not always easy to respond in the moment to a helpee, or anyone else for that matter. Perhaps you had some difficulty responding to the young woman. Following training, you will be able to rate your own response to this young woman.

Now, to give you an idea of how well you can judge helpful responses, we will consider several alternative responses that might have been made by someone trying to help this person. Next to each of the responses, you should write a number to indicate your rating of the effectiveness of that response. Use the following rating scale.

1—Very Ineffective
2—Ineffective
3—Minimally Effective
4—Very Effective
5—Extremely Effective

Your Ratings   **Helper Responses**

_____ 1. *"You're saying you don't know what major to choose and nobody has been able to help you find your direction."*

_____ 2. *"Engineering is a pretty rough field — particulary for a woman."*

_____ 3. *"You really feel mixed up because your parents want one thing and you're interested in another, and worst of all, no one's helping you sort things out."*

_____ 4. *"You feel upset with yourself because you don't know how to make this important decision and you want to be able to make a good choice. A first step might be for us to list your most important personal values that will be affected by this decision and see how the alternatives stack up against your values."*

_____ 5. *"You're feeling helpless and sorta' angry at yourself because you just don't know how to weigh things out in this situation, and you really want to make the right decision."*

Discriminating Helpful Responses

Now check your ratings against the expert ratings of these responses.

Response #2 was rated 1 because it was totally irrelevant to the helpee's expression. Response # 1 was rated 2 because it was directly related to what the helpee said, but it did not respond to the feelings expressed by the helpee. Response #3 was rated 3 because it was an accurate response to where the helpee is in terms of both content and feelings expressed. Such a response communicates the helper's understanding, but it does not go beyond this understanding to provide direction for the helpee.

Response #5 was rated 4 because it was an accurate response to both where the helpee is and where she wants to be (". . . *you really want to make the right decision . . .*"). The response fell short of a 5 rating because it did not identify a specific first step towards the helpee's goal.

Response #4 was rated 5 because it was an accurate response to where the helpee is, where she wants to be and how to get from where she is to where she wants to be. By suggesting a specific first step that the helpee could take toward the achievement of her goal, this response provided both understanding and concrete direction.

Receiving Feedback

To calculate your pre-test **discrimination** score, do the following things.

1. Without regard to whether the difference is positive or negative, write down the difference between each of your numerical ratings and each of the experts' numerical ratings.
2. Add up the difference scores. You should have five scores, one for each response alternative.
3. Divide the total of the difference scores by 5. The result is your pre-test discrimination score.

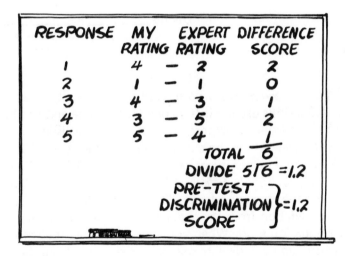

RESPONSE	MY RATING		EXPERT RATING	DIFFERENCE SCORE
1	4	–	2	2
2	1	–	1	0
3	4	–	3	1
4	3	–	5	2
5	5	–	4	1

TOTAL 6
DIVIDE 5⟌6 = 1.2
PRE-TEST DISCRIMINATION SCORE } = 1.2

Calculating

Response	Your Rating		Expert Rating		Difference Between Ratings
1	_____	–	2	=	_____
2	_____	–	1	=	_____
3	_____	–	3	=	_____
4	_____	–	5	=	_____
5	_____	–	4	=	_____

Total = _____

Divide _____ = _____

5   *Your Pre-Training Discrimination Score*

The average person who has not had systematic training in helping skills usually differs one (1.0) to one-and-one-half (1.5) levels from the experts' ratings. This is really not good since it means where the experts rated an item at level 3 the untrained helper might rate the response 4.5 or 1.5. You are rating as *"Highly Effective"* or *"Highly Ineffective"* a response that the expert rates *"Minimally Effective."* A half-a-level deviation from the expert scores is considered a good discrimination score. When you have completed the work in this book you will deviate one-half level or less from the experts' ratings.

You are just beginning your helping journey. When you have mastered all of the helping skills in this book, you will be ready to come back and rate your own response to the helpee in order to obtain your pre-test **communication** score.

Even now, however, you may be able to get a pretty good idea of your current level of helping skills by comparing your response to the other five response alternatives.

A more detailed discussion of the communication rating scale will be presented later in this book.

You start here.

Beginning

2

attending

In their early months, infants require a great deal of attention. They must be nursed and fed. They must be clothed and changed. They must be held and loved. All of these acts attend to their basic needs. All of these acts prepare them for life.

By attending to their physical needs, we assure them of survival. By attending to their emotional needs, we free them to experience themselves in relation to their worlds. By attending to their intellectual needs, we free them to experiment with themselves and learn about themselves in relation to their worlds.

When infants call for attention and they receive it, they learn perhaps the most important message of all. They learn that they can have an impact upon their world.

In a similar manner, we establish the basis for helping by attending to the person in need of help. Basically, attending involves some physical act on the part of the helper. Through some physical act, the helper enables the helpee to become involved in a helping process by expressing herself freely to another person. Generally, attending can be defined as being attentive to the helpee. Attending is made up of attending physically, observing and listening to the helpee.

Attending

Before we begin to learn attending skills, let us take stock of how you attend and have been attended to in your life. How do people who really care about you communicate attention to you? Conversely, how can you tell that people **are not** paying attention to you? What do they do physically? If someone is talking about something very important to them, how do you communicate to them that you are really interested?

Similarly, when you are observing people while attending to them, what do you look for? What gives you cues about what is going on inside of them? Have you ever been really nervous about something very important? What do you do that tells people that you are upset?

Further, when you are listening to others, what do you listen for? What tells you what is really important to the other person? How do you know what the "real problem" is? If something is really bothering you, how do you emphasize your point? How do you express yourself? What words do you use?

The answers to these questions lead directly to learning the attending skills that involve the helpee in helping.

Attending Involves the Helpee

ATTENDING PHYSICALLY

Attending physically encompasses involving the helpee and attending contextually and personally to the helpee. **Involving the helpee** includes informing the helpee of your availability and readiness to help and encouraging the helpee to use that help. When informing formal clients, you will want to invite the helpee to her helping interview by inform- ing her (in person, by phone or in writing) of the basic facts: **who** she will be seeing; **when** and **where** the appointment will take place; **how** to get there; and **what** the general purpose of the interview will be.

You may tell informal helpees of your availability and readiness to help in less structured ways. You might invite a colleague to lunch, or invite a neighbor over to talk, or take a walk with a friend. In other words, you only need to inform the person about **when** and **where.**

I'd like to get together.
How about going to
lunch today?

Attending Physically

Information, of course, is not enough to get a helpee involved in a helping process. People often need motivation as well as information if they are going to share their experiences with another person.

Encouraging is the second step in involving a helpee in a helping process. Encouraging means giving the helpee a personal reason to become involved.

Encouraging should take place at the same time as informing the helpee. It should include telling the helpee about a potential benefit of getting involved in helping. It should also express your personal interest in working with the helpee. You answer the helpee's question, *"Why should I get involved?"* At the same time you indicate your own willingness to get involved.

You should practice your informing and encouraging skills with people you meet. It does not even have to be for helping purposes. You can simply invite and encourage someone to come for a visit or a group get-together.

We have a lot of helpful
information over here...
I'll be glad to work
with you.

Involving

When we involve the helpee in helping, we bring her into the helping environment or the context in which helping takes place. Here we attend to her through the context of helping. **Attending contextually** refers to arranging the helping environment to communicate the helper's interest and support for the helpee.

We may communicate interest and attentiveness simply by the way we arrange furniture in the helping setting. The helper and helpee should sit in chairs which face each other, four to five feet apart, with no desks, tables or other barriers between them. This arrangement communicates an openness and readiness on the helper's part to become involved with the helpee. It will put the helper in a position to fully see and hear the helpee.

If there are several helpees, the chairs should be placed in a circle. This physical arrangement will facilitate the helpees communicating interest and attentiveness to each other. The arrangement will also allow the helper to communicate interest and attentiveness. However, the helper will need to be conscious of shifting her body position to face fully the helpee who is speaking at any particular moment. Finally, the helper and helpee chairs should be of the same height to communicate equality and partnership rather than authority and power.

Attending Contextually

Attending contextually also involves displaying decorations and using materials with which the helpee can identify. Rather than being strange and distracting, these objects in the helping setting should reflect the helpee's world and make the helpee feel welcome. For example, if you have formal or informal helpees who are college students, your decorations and materials should reflect things that are familiar to college students.

In addition, the helping setting should be organized and orderly, indicating that the helper is on top of her own affairs and ready to focus her attention on the helpee. You can develop your contextual attending skills by arranging your office or a room where you live so that it is conducive to relating to others and making them feel comfortable.

Identifying

By involving and attending contextually to the helpee, we bring her into close proximity with us as helpers. This allows us to attend to the helpee personally.

Attending personally may involve meeting the helpee's immediate physical needs as well as posturing yourself physically to communicate interest and attentiveness.

We may actually need to attend to some very basic physical needs of the helpee. If, for example, the helpee has not eaten in some time, we may offer her food. We may offer her nourishment by literally sharing physical nutrition. Symbolically, we may accomplish the same end by offering her a glass of milk or a cup of tea or coffee.

In the same manner, we offer the helpee the protection of the physical setting for helping. If she is harrassed and anxious, we may offer her the sanctuary of solitude. Symbolically, our provision of a supportive setting and a degree of real attention may offer her a brief respite from a world that seems to be rapidly closing in on her.

Attending Personally

How we posture ourselves is a critical part of attending personally. Our posture communicates our readiness to respond to the helpee's needs. Our thoughts and feelings often reflect our posture. When we posture ourselves for others, we tend to think of others. When we posture ourselves for our own comfort and convenience, we tend to think of ourselves.

Posturing

One way of posturing ourselves to attend to the helpee is to face her fully. Whether standing or sitting, we may turn to the helpee and face her squarely—our left shoulder to her right shoulder and *vice versa.* When we are dealing with a couple or a small group of people, we should place ourselves at the point of a right angle drawn from the people to our extreme left and right. See how differently we feel about the helpee when we posture ourselves in this manner from how we feel when we posture ourselves for our own purposes.

Squaring

There are other ways of posturing ourselves to attend
personally. The inclination of our bodies is one critical way.
For example, when we are sitting we attend most fully when
we incline our bodies forward or toward the helpee to a
point where we can rest our forearms on our thighs. When
standing, we attend most fully when we close the physical
distance by moving closer to the helpee. Putting one leg in
front of the other will help us to lean slightly toward the
helpee.

There are still other ways of attending to a person in need
of help.

Leaning

We must seek in every way possible to communicate our full and undivided attention. Perhaps the key way of attending personally involves how we use our senses, particularly our eyes. We communicate attentiveness when we maintain eye contact with the helpee. The helpee is aware of our efforts to make contact with her psychologically through our efforts to make contact with her visually.

Eyeing

The helper communicates personal attending by all of her mannerisms and expressions. When she is intense but relaxed, she communicates attentiveness. When she is nervous and fidgety, she communicates that she doesn't want to be there. When she is consistent in attentive behavior, she communicates her interest. When she blushes or turns pale, she communicates different levels of reaction to the helpee. The helper must have herself *"together"* in her attending behavior.

You can practice your own attending posture, first in front of a mirror and then with people you see in everyday life to whom you want to communicate interest and concern. You may feel awkward at first; after awhile, however, you should notice that you focus more on the other person and that she is more attentive to you.

Communicating Interest

One way of structuring attending physically while sitting is to view yourself in terms of the skills involved. Indeed, you may rate yourself as follows according to your demonstration of the skills:

High attending — Squared, eyeing and leaning 20° or more
Moderate attending — Squared, eyeing
Low attending — Non-facing or slouching

Low

Moderate

High

Levels of Physical Attending While Sitting

Clearly, you do not always attend physically by sitting. Often, you are attempting to help people when you are standing. You can use a similar scale to rate your demonstration of the skills while standing:

High attending - Squared, eyeing and leaning 10°
Moderate attending — Squared, eyeing
Low attending — Non-facing

Levels of Physical Attending While Standing

Now we are going to assign you your first helpee. You are going to work with him in the very same developmental way that we have described in the introduction to this book.

We are going to **develop** the helping relationship through the helpee stages of exploration, understanding and action, and we are going to deal with some real-life problems. In doing so, however, we want to keep the focus upon the helping skills (attending, responding, personalizing, initiating) and not the problems. Specific problem areas will be dealt with in greater detail in later works.

Tom is a neighbor. He's a young adult. Sort of slow moving but intelligent. He really doesn't know where he is going or what he is going to do. But he asks a lot of good questions. He is searching. Searching to be understood. Searching to understand.

He hangs around your place a lot. Seems he feels as if you might answer some of his questions. Maybe he hopes that you can understand. Maybe he hopes that you can help him understand.

Tom

Your first task is to attend to Tom. Involve him, attend to him contextually, attend to him personally.

To involve Tom, you will want to inform him of your availability and interest in helping him, encouraging him to take a first step toward being helped by you. What could you say to involve Tom and encourage him to talk with you? You may need to repeat your invitation several times and/or vary your encouragement.

Once Tom has agreed to talk with you, you will need to attend contextually to him to further communicate your interest and attentiveness. What kind of a place would you choose? Hopefully one that is quiet and free of distractions.

Finally, you will attend personally to Tom. You are sitting opposite each other. Take a look at yourself right now. See how you posture yourself. How much openness do you communicate? How much receptiveness?

See yourself through Tom's eyes. Ask Tom's questions:
"Is this a person who is open to me?"
"Can I share?"
"Do I dare ask my real questions?"

I've been thinking about some of the things you said....

Attending to Tom

OBSERVING

When we attend to a helpee, we position ourselves to pay attention to the helpee. When we pay attention to the helpee, we increase the input that we get through observing her. Observing skills involve the helper's ability to see and understand the nonverbal behavior of the helpee. These skills are essential because the richest source of empathy is the helper's observation of the helpee's physical behavior. We must observe those aspects of the helpee's appearance and behavior which tell us about the helpee's energy level, her feeling and her degree of congruence (whether she really is as she appears). The helpee gives us many cues to her experience in her physical behavior and appearance. When all other cues to the helpee's experience confuse us, we must return to the most basic evidence of all—the helpee's behavior.

Attending Physically Observing

The chief physical characteristic of any person is her energy level. When an individual's energy level is low, she functions poorly. When an individual's energy level is high, she is more apt to function effectively.

Knowing how long the individual can sustain high levels of functioning is essential if we are to know how she experiences her life. An individual's energy level enables her to follow through on achieving goals in the face of adverse circumstances. An individual's energy level allows her to experience the fullness of life. Persons with low energy levels have great difficulty in meeting even the simplest demands of everyday life.

Observing Energy Level

When an individual is alive and eager to live each day, she is physically active in living fully each day. Children are usually alive and full of energy. When they are not full of life, they are often suffering from some illness, physical or psychological.

Unlike the healthy child, however, many helpees often function at low levels of physical energy. Because of conflicts within them, their energies are drained. They appear fatigued, are slow to respond and often respond inappropriately to the situation. Everything is a burden and they experience their day-to-day routine as overwhelming. Even when they function periodically at high levels, they are unable to sustain this behavior for prolonged periods of time.

Observing Health

In observing for energy level, there are four specific areas on which to focus your observations: body build, posture, grooming and nonverbal expressions. Observations in each area should be limited to objectively verifiable visual cues.

In terms of energy level, helpees who are significantly overweight or underweight and/or whose muscle tone is poor will tend to have lower levels of energy.

Energy level is also communicated by the alertness of the helpee's posture. Specifically, the helper will look for the same cues in the helpee that were discussed earlier in helper attending: the extent to which the helpee stands and sits erect or inclined forward with eyes focused on the helper. The helpee who sits slouched in her seat with shoulders drooped is taking a position that suggests low energy.

Cues to the helpee's energy level can also be observed in her grooming and nonverbal expression. It takes a certain amount of energy to maintain a clean and neat appearance. By the same token, nonverbal expressions like a slack face or slow movements are frequently indicative of a helpee's low level of physical energy.

Check out:
build, posture,
grooming, expressions.

Observing Appearance and Behavior

These same four areas of body build, posture, grooming and nonverbal expression are also the focus of observations for feelings. While posture and nonverbal expression, particularly facial expression, are the richest sources of data concerning the helpee's feelings, the other areas can also contribute to understanding the helpee's experience. For example, poor grooming may indicate a *"down"* feeling. At another level, a large, strong male helpee may be more prone to feelings of shame at his inability to handle his distress.

There are many other indices of behavior which give us cues to the person's inner experience. Think of how different behavioral cues tell us how a person feels. Think of our own behaviors which reflect different feeling states.

Observing Identifies Feelings

When there are discrepancies in a person's behavior or appearance, we say that she is incongruent. Being incongruent simply means that the person is not consistent in different aspects of her behavior or appearance. For example, the person may say she feels fine while sitting slumped in her chair, looking at the floor and fidgeting.

Being incongruent is itself a critical sign of a person in trouble. Responding to incongruencies may be appropriate when done from a base of understanding. We will learn how to do this most effectively in the section on personalizing. But first we must communicate our understanding of the helpee's frame of reference.

Remember that the helpee invariably wants to become more positively congruent. Perhaps the most important aspect of behavior to which we can respond initially is the helpee's desire to get herself *"together."* The fact is that, more than anything in the world, she wants to be able to function capably without those glaring inconsistencies in her effectiveness.

Observing the Degree of Congruence

Accurately observing the helpee's behavior is part of the helping effort. We are helping the helpee to increase the consistency in her behaviors—the consistency between her physical and verbal behaviors and between both these types of behavior and the helpee's real experience of herself.

It is important to practice observing behavior. We must attempt to determine what experience the behavior expresses. If we do not notice or if we ignore helpee behavior, the helpee is unlikely to explore her real feelings and her real problems fully.

Helping must also mean not hurting. If a helpee is not ready to accept or deal with an observation, then that observation should not be expressed. In this regard, it should be noted that observations must be considered hypotheses, to be confirmed or denied over time by the helpee's behavioral and verbal expressions. Observations should not be taken as a valid basis for making snap judgments about a person.

Observing Accurately

Now take a good look at Tom. Based on appearance, it would seem that his energy level is moderate. On the one hand he is neat and clean and is sitting forward in his chair. His height is also in proportion to his weight. On the other hand, his slack facial muscles would indicate a low level of energy at the moment. And his down-turned mouth suggests a *"down"* kind of feeling. Finally, Tom's behavior does appear congruent with his words. His facial expression indicates that he is really experiencing the fact that things are not going well.

Things are not going so good for me.

Observing Tom

One way of structuring observing is to observe the helpees for precisely the same attending posture which you tried to exhibit as helpers. These observational inferences will help guide you in interpreting the behavior you are observing. You can complement these inferences with the richness of other observations. You can make inferences about the helpee's functioning from these data as follows:

	Low Attending	Moderate Attending	High Attending
Areas	⬇	⬇	⬇
Physical	Low Energy	Moderate Energy	High Energy
Emotional	Down Feelings	Mixed Feelings	Up Feelings
Intellectual	Low Readiness	Moderate Readiness	High Readiness

Levels of Observational Inferences

Now take a moment and look at yourself. What does your appearance and behavior say about you? Do you project a high energy level? What do your posture and behavior say about your feelings right now? Is your posture congruent with your expressed desire to learn about helping? You can sharpen your own observing skills by trying to size up the energy level, feelings and degree of congruence of the people whom you encounter in your daily living. It is particularly important to do this with people with whom you are trying to establish a constructive relationship, be they helpees, friends or loved ones.

Observing Yourself

LISTENING

Along with the helpee's behavioral expressions, the helpee's verbal expressions are also a very rich source of empathy. What people say and how they say it tells us a lot about how they see themselves and the world around them.

When we give the helpee our full and undivided attention, we have prepared ourselves for listening to the helpee. The more we attend physically to the helpee, the better we can listen to the cues reflecting her inner experience. The more we observe the helpee, the more we prepare ourselves for listening to her. There are many ways that we can develop our listening skills.

What will she say,
and
How will she say it?

Observing ▶ Listening

First, the helper-as-listener should know why she is there. We should have a reason for listening. We should know what we are looking for. If we are going to help, we should be establishing a relationship that makes helping possible.

As with observing, we should be listening for cues to the helpee's feelings, level of energy and degree of congruence. We should also be listening for the *"who, what, when, where, why and how"* *(5W*H*)* of the situation. To do this, we must focus not only on the words but also on the tone of voice.

Reason for listening.

Knowing What to Listen For

Next, it is important to suspend our own personal judgment in listening, at least initially. If we are going to listen to what the helpee has to say, we must temporarily suspend the things which we say to ourselves. We must let the helpee's message sink in without trying to make decisions about it.

Suspend own judgment.

Being Nonjudgmental

Perhaps the most important thing in listening is to resist distractions. Just as we initially resist the judgmental voice within ourselves so we must also resist outside distractions. There will always be a lot of things going on that will not help us to listen. We must place ourselves in such a way as to avoid noises, views, people—anything or anyone that will take us away from the person to whom we are listening.

Resisting Distractions

Now recall the content of Tom's expression.

"Things are not going so good for me. Not in school. Not with my girl. I just seem to be floundering. I fake it every day but inside I'm really down because I'm not sure of what I want to do or where I want to go."

Can you find the cues to Tom's feelings, energy level and congruence? Can you find any cues as to who's involved, what's happening, when and where it happens, why and how it happens? Some of the cues the helpee gives are direct. For example, Tom says explicitly that he feels down. Other cues are only implied. The fact that Tom can still fake it every day implies a fairly high energy level—even though this energy is being drained away. Other cues may not be present at all. Tom makes no mention of when and where his problems with his girl take place. These *"gaps"* in the helpee's exploration can become the basis for later questions if the helpee does not voluntarily introduce the information.

You can practice your listening skills by finding other expressions made to you during the course of your interactions with others and practice recalling the content and tone of the expression.

Feelings, energy, congruence, 5 WH?

Recalling the Expression

So far we have just focused on listening to each statement as the helpee presents it. But we must also learn to recall helpee expressions over a period of time.

The helpee's important themes will be repeated over and over and with the most intensity. The speaker will make the same points over and over in different ways. The themes will tell us what the speaker is really trying to say about herself in relation to her world. She will tell us where she is *"coming from"* if we just provide her the opportunity.

Look for common themes.

Looking for Themes

There is no question that listening is hard work and requires intense concentration. But remember this: just as there are different rates for reading, so there are also different rates for listening. Most speakers talk at a rate between 100 and 150 words a minute. Yet we can easily listen at a rate of two or three times that. We can put this extra time to use by reflecting upon or thinking about what the helpee has said.

Reflecting on What Is Said

Remember, most of us have been taught not to listen or to hear. Years of conditioning have gone into this. We are distracted because we do not want to hear. We distort the expressions because of the implications of understanding. Most of all, there are the implications for intimacy that people are fearful of. So just as we have been conditioned not to listen or hear, now we must train ourselves to actively listen and hear.

I want to hear.

Hearing

One way of structuring listening is to test your verbatim recall of the helpee's expression. Simply listen to the next expression that you hear, whether a live interaction or otherwise. Then try to repeat verbatim what you heard. Rate your accuracy of recall as follows:

High accuracy — Verbatim recall of expression

Moderate accuracy — Recall of gist of expression

Low accuracy — Little or no recall of expression

Levels of Listening

Now you can begin to build your own cumulative rating scale for helping. If the helper is attending physically and observing and listening to the helpee, you may rate the helper as fully attentive (level 2.0). If the helper is only attending physically, then the helper is rated at less than fully attentive levels (level 1.5). If the helper is not attending physically, then the helper cannot be rated in relation to the helpee (level 1.0).

5.0
4.5
4.0
3.5
3.0
2.5
2.0 Observing and listening
1.5 Attending physically
1.0 Non-attending

Levels of Helping: Attending

If you have attended to Tom appropriately—attending physically, observing and listening to him—he will feel comfortable. He will be able to answer his questions affirmatively.

"This is a person who appears open to me."

"I think I can share."

"I may even be able to ask the things that are really on my mind."

To be sure, Tom's answers are cautious. But this is appropriate, for you have not met the real tests yet.

Most important, Tom is responding to you. You have reached out. And he is reaching back—however tentatively.

The helping process is initiated.

Involving the Helpee

If you have not attended to Tom appropriately, he will not feel comfortable. He will not be able to answer his questions affirmatively. Instead, his answers tell him to move away.

"This does not appear to be a person who is open to me!"

"I don't think I can share."

"I won't be able to ask the things that are really on my mind."

Again, Tom's answers are tentative. They are not forever. They are not irreversible. But they do reflect his initial impression of your initial behavior.

Most important, Tom is not responding to you. Quite the opposite, he is pulling back.

The helping process has not been initiated.

I don't think she can help.

Not Involving the Helpee

Of course, you may not wish to help Tom. You may not wish to relate to many people in your life in a helping manner. And many of them will not wish you to do so.

Your attending behavior will tell them whether you wish to help or not.

If Tom does not find you helpful, he must look elsewhere. If he cannot find assistance anywhere else, he may have to seek professional help. He may have to pay for the kind of human attention that he cannot find in his everyday life.

But even here, the professional helper or counselor may or may not attend appropriately to Tom's needs. She may reach Tom or she may turn Tom away. If she turns Tom away, Tom is without help. He is doomed to search alone, without the help of others unless he is fortunate enough to meet someone like the person you might have been for him— someone who is a helper.

Involving Yourself

The effective helper will reach Tom. She won't seat herself as if she is a queen on a high throne indulging her underling. She will give Tom her full physical and psychological attention. She will face Tom fully. She will lean slightly forward, toward Tom. And she will maintain eye contact with Tom. Above all, she will use her attending skills to observe and listen to Tom and to develop tentative hypotheses based on his physical and verbal behavior.

Tom will feel secure and comfortable. He will involve himself in a helping process that might change the course of his life for the better.

Demonstrating Attending Skills

You might continue to practice your attending behaviors with your friends. This is the way you prepare them for involvement with you. This is the way you reach out to them. You might also check yourself out by eliciting their responses to your behavior. You should find that you have reached them.

With trusted persons who will not in any way get hurt, you might also try the opposite behavior. You might try out *"nonattentive"* behaviors and check out their effects upon these other persons. For example, you might posture yourself in a slouch with your back to the person and your eyes fixed upon some other object in the room. You should find that the person is less involved with you.

When our helpees are turned from our doorstep in this manner, we may sentence them to an endless search for help elsewhere.

Practicing Attending Skills

Again, the function of attending to helpees is to give them the feelings of security that make their involvement in the helping process possible. When they have begun to express material that they feel is relevant for them, they have signaled their readiness for us to communicate our understanding of their explorations. In order to facilitate their exploration of personally relevant and important material, we as helpers must use our responding skills.

Preparing for Responding

3

responding

One of the critical characteristics that separates human beings from other species of life is their facility for verbal expression. One of the critical characteristics that separates children from infants is their increasing facility for verbal expression.

Children can express themselves in many different ways. They can express themselves in their physical behavior. They can express themselves in their verbal behavior.

We can respond to children's experiences in many different ways. We can respond to them in our physical behavior. We can respond to them in our verbal behavior.

We can meet children's needs by our physical and verbal responses. For example, we can lie down on the bed with a distraught child and hold her. We can also respond verbally to the level of distress which she is experiencing.

Similarly, in helping we can encourage our helpees' expressions by responding to their experiences in many different ways. As we have seen, we can respond to them in our physical behavior. As we will learn in this chapter, we can also respond with our verbal behavior. The helper does this through responding to the helpee's expression of her experience. Responding involves responding to content, feeling and feeling and content together.

Responding

Before we go on to learn responding skills, let us take stock of how you respond and have been responded to in your life. Once you have attended to the helpees and involved them in the helping process, what do you do with what they give you? What do you do with what you have observed and listened to?

What do you say that makes them feel that you really understood them? Since you have received information from them, what can you say to them in return to assure them of your understanding? Conversely, when you shared a problem with someone, what did that person say to you that showed you that he or she really understood you?

The answers to these questions lead directly to learning the responding skills that facilitate the helpee's exploration of where he or she is in helping.

You feel
upset.

Responding Facilitates Helpee Exploration

RESPONDING TO CONTENT

We listen to the helpee so that we can respond to her. We respond first to the most obvious part of her expression—the content.

When we respond to content, we can respond verbally as well as physically to the helpee. Indeed, one of the critical ways in which the helpee can tell if the helper is hearing her is to check out the verbal responses of the helper.

By responding to content, we begin to communicate our understanding of the helpee's experience. Another word for this communication of understanding is *"empathy."*

Empathy is a word which we use when one individual is hearing or understanding another. Empathy involves crawling inside another person's skin and seeing the world through her eyes. The Indians used to talk of *"walking in another's moccasins."* **Empathy involves experiencing another person's world as if you were she.**

What if I were her?

Listening Responding to Content

In effect, the helper attempts to merge temporarily with the helpee. The helper merges with the helpee so that both may explore the helpee's experience. Together, helper and helpee attempt to explore all details of the helpee's experience—the nooks and crannies as well as the big picture.

The helper can facilitate this empathic understanding by encouraging and rewarding specificity in the helpee's expressions. The more specific the helpee is about her experiences, the more empathic the helper can be. The more the helpee can describe specific events, the more accurate the helper can be in her understanding.

Spell it all out.

Being Specific

We can best understand the helpee's frame of reference by suspending our attitudes which might prevent her from sharing herself or prevent us from entering her world. We can share the helpee's frame of reference only by temporarily suspending our own frame of reference.

At this stage of helping, then, we communicate respect for the helpee's frame of reference by suspending our own. In this way, the helpee has the feeling that she is free to explore herself without fear of retaliation. No matter what she does or says, no harm will come to her.

Suspending Our Own Frame of Reference

While suspending our own frame of reference, we must continue to communicate in a genuine manner. This does **not** mean that we dominate the helping process with our free expressions of ourselves. We cannot be fully and freely ourselves for what we present may be overwhelming for the helpee. **Helping is for the helpee.**

What being genuine does mean is that we do not present ourselves in a phony manner. At the very minimum, we present no facade that would misrepresent ourselves. We present no mask from a professional or other role that might make the helpee uncomfortable and unable to share herself.

Presenting No Phoniness

The skill of responding to content involves being able to communicate an accurate understanding of the unique situation as presented by another. A good response to content is based upon carefully listening to the details presented by the helpee. However, the response formulated by the helper does not need to repeat these details. Rather, the response should be as brief a summary as possible. That is, it should not ramble or contain any nonessential elements. This will help to ensure that the helpee can clearly hear your understanding. Finally, a good response rephrases the helpee's expression in a fresh way. It does not simply *"parrot"* back the helpee's own words. A good format for doing this is *"You're saying _____"* or *"In other words _____ ."*

Responding to Content

Now let us try to formulate a response to Tom's expression. Let us repeat the content of the expression again:

"Things are not going so good for me. Not in school. Not with my girl. I just seem to be floundering. I fake it every day but inside I'm really down because I'm not sure of what I want to do or where I want to go."

We have again reflected on the content. Now we formulate a response: *"You're saying that you're lost and just going through the motions—with your girl and with your schooling."*

You should practice responding to the content presented to you by other people in your life, particularly those who are important to you. You will find that it will encourage their opening up their experiences to you at a fuller level.

Practicing Responding to Content

RESPONDING TO FEELINGS

Just as we showed our empathy for the helpee by responding to the content of her expression, so we may also show our understanding of the helpee's experience by responding to the feelings of the helpee. Indeed, responding to content prepares us to respond to the feeling of the helpee's expression.

Helpees may express verbally and directly those feelings which dominate them. Or the helpees may only express their feelings indirectly through their tone of voice or by describing the situation in which they find themselves.

Whether the helpee's expression is direct or indirect, our goal as helpers will be to show the helpee explicitly our level of understanding of her feelings. This will give the helpee a chance to check out our ability as helpers. It will give us a chance to check ourselves out.

From what she says, she must feel bad.

Responding to Content ▶ Responding to Feelings

To respond to the helpee's feelings, we must do several things. First, as we have learned, we must observe her behavior. In particular, we must pay attention to her posture and facial expressions. How the helpee expresses herself will tell us a great deal about how she experiences herself. Her tone of voice and her facial expressions will be valuable clues to her inner feelings.

She sure looks like it was a rough experience.

Observing the Helpee's Behavior and Presentation

Next we must listen carefully to the helpee's words. When we have listened to her words, we must summarize what we have seen and heard that is indicative of the helpee's feelings. Then we ask ourselves the question *"If I were the helpee and I were doing and saying these things, how would I feel?"* In answering this question, you can first identify the general feeling category (happy, angry, sad, confused, scared, strong or weak) and the intensity of the feeling (high, medium or low). Then select a feeling word or phrase that fits the feeling area and level of intensity. Finally check out the feeling expression with your observations to see if it is appropriate for the helpee. (For example, it would not be appropriate to use the word *"morose"* to capture the feeling of gloom of most clients with a sixth-grade education.)

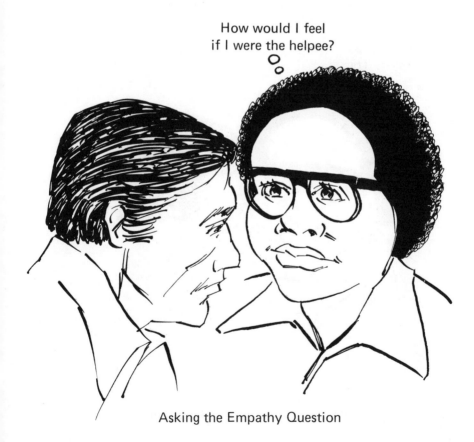

How would I feel
if I were the helpee?

Asking the Empathy Question

Now we can try to understand the feelings expressed by Tom. Summarize the cues to Tom's feelings and then ask and answer the question *"How would I feel if I were Tom and were saying these things?"*

"Things are not going so good for me. Not in school. Not with my girl. I just seem to be floundering. I fake it every day but inside I'm really down because I'm not sure of what I want to do or where I want to go."

The main cue to Tom's feeling is that he says he feels down. He's down about school and down about his relationship with his girl. He's also floundering. If we were in Tom's position, we might very well feel sad.

Practice asking and answering to yourself the *"How would I feel?"* question with other expressions that you hear in everyday life.

Answering the Empathy Question

We may say that we respond to the helpees' feelings when we capture the essence of their feelings in one or more feeling words. To capture another person's feeling, then, we need to know a lot of feeling words. We need to develop a feeling-word vocabulary. It is not enough to understand what the helpee is saying. **We must also communicate to the helpees our understanding of their feelings.**

Developing Feeling Words

We can ensure that we respond to the helpee's feelings when we make a response that is interchangeable with the feelings expressed by the helpee. **It certainly is not too much to expect that we at least be able to communicate to helpees what they have communicated to us.** Understanding what the helpees have expressed—at **the level they have expressed it**—constitutes the only basis for helping.

A response is interchangeable if both the helper and the helpee express the same feeling. In operation this means that, in terms of the feelings expressed, the helper could have said what the helpee said and the helpee could have said what the helper said.

Developing Interchangeable Responses

The first responses which we formulate should involve very simple feeling words reflecting the feelings expressed by the helpee. We may do this by using a simple *"You feel ____ _____"* formulation. Before we move to more complex communication, we must learn to formulate simple responses.

"You feel
_____."

Responding to Feelings

Now let us try to formulate a feeling response to Tom's expression. Let us repeat his expression again:

"Things are not going so good for me. Not in school. Not with my girl. I just seem to be floundering. I fake it every day. But inside I'm really down because I'm not sure of what I want to do or where I want to go."

Again, we have asked ourselves *"How would I feel if I were Tom?"* We answer *"Sad—I would feel sad."* Now we formulate the response in a way that we can communicate directly to Tom how **he** feels: *"You feel sad."*

You feel sad.

Responding to Sad Feelings

As you have found, Tom has exhibited many different moods—many different feeling states. Sometimes he seems very sad. Sometimes he seems very happy. Sometimes he seems very angry. Most times he is somewhere in between these extremes.

We must have responses which communicate to him our understanding in each of these moments. Formulate simple responses to each of Tom's feeling states.

One of the feelings that seems to dominate Tom is a kind of sad or *"down"* feeling. His energy level appears low. Things seem pretty hopeless. He feels helpless in the face of everything. He just does not know where he is going or whether he can get there. Sometimes he verbalizes this feeling: *"Sometimes I just think that I'm not going to make it."*

Using the appropriate feeling word for this kind of sadness, you might formulate a simple response.

You feel discouraged.

Responding Accurately

In rare moments, Tom might be *"up,"* particularly when he has found some direction—however tentative. His whole demeanor changes. His attitude toward life opens up. His behavior is intense and rapid.

It is just as important to be able to respond to Tom in these moments as it is to respond to him in his depressed moments. Indeed, it is ultimately more important.

While it is critical to pick Tom up at the level that he is expressing himself, we must ultimately help him to move to new and more rewarding behavior. We cannot help him to move if we cannot respond to those rare moments of joy.

For many of us, these are the most difficult experiences to respond to. To share another's joy is difficult indeed for those of us whose own moments of joy are few and far between.

Sometimes Tom's feelings are so intense that he blurts them out: *"I'm just so eager and excited—I can't wait to get started."*

You might formulate a simple response to Tom's feeling state.

You feel really great.

Responding to Happy Feelings

At other times, Tom might express other kinds of feelings which might be difficult to respond to. Sometimes he is just mad at the world, angry with its injustice and motivated to retaliate. His body is tense, his eyes tearing and his expressions choked. Often we are afraid to open up such feelings. We are afraid to unleash a tide which we cannot later stem. We are afraid of how far these feelings may carry Tom. *"Will he act upon them?" "Will he act them out?"* These are the questions which characterize our concern.

Nevertheless, we cannot help if we cannot deal with all of a person's feelings. Tom must get these feelings out in the open if he is going to learn to deal with them. Indeed, the probability of his acting upon hateful feelings is inversely related to his ability to explore them: the more he explores them, the less likely he is to act destructively. Put another way, the more he explores them the more likely he is to channel them constructively. Sometimes Tom expresses his feelings in violent terms: *"I know damn well I'm going to get back at him any way I can."*

Formulate a simple response to him.

You feel furious.

Responding to Angry Feelings

We must respond to Tom in all his fullness. In his moments of sadness, happiness and anger. He **is** how he feels.

If we do not respond to him in his fullness, the implications are clear: if we cannot find him, we lose him. If we lose him, he cannot find himself.

There are many unique feelings that could be used to capture Tom's experiences. Practice formulating at least 10 feeling words each for the feeling states of sadness, happiness and anger. See if you can determine what kinds of expressions by the helpee might call for using any one of these words.

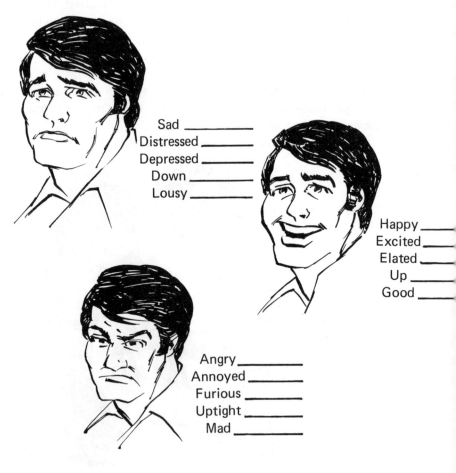

Sad _____
Distressed _____
Depressed _____
Down _____
Lousy _____

Happy _____
Excited _____
Elated _____
Up _____
Good _____

Angry _____
Annoyed _____
Furious _____
Uptight _____
Mad _____

Responding to Unique Feelings

In addition, there are many variations of these feeling state themes. Other major themes are confusion, fright, strength and weakness. There are a wide range of feeling states to which we can respond.

We must learn to respond to these unique feelings. It is beneficial for both the helper and the helpee to struggle to capture in words the uniqueness of the helpee's experience.

When Tom has lost his direction and expresses himself in this manner—*"I just don't know which way to turn"*—you might respond to his loss of direction. Try formulating a number of words which capture the uniqueness of his experience.

You feel confused.
You feel _____.

Responding to Other Feelings

The more feeling words which you have available, the better your chances of matching the words up with Tom's unique experience.

When Tom finds himself in a situation where he feels his insides tugged and offers *"I feel like I am getting pulled both ways,"* you might respond to his inner struggle.

You feel torn.
You feel_____

When Tom is simply unable to express himself, you might respond to this inability.

You feel blocked.
You feel _____.

The More Feeling Words You Know...

One effective way of organizing feeling words is to categorize them according to whether they are of high, medium or low intensity. Since the intensity of any word depends upon the person with whom it is used, you will need to visualize the typical helpee you work with to categorize by intensity level. Then you can discriminate both the feeling category and the level of intensity which you wish to employ. Develop your own word list by filling in the next page. Appendix A contains an alphabetical listing of feeling words for you to draw from. Carry your list around with you. Add to it. It will help you respond accurately.

You are struggling for the right words.

. . . the Easier It Will Be to Respond Accurately . . .

Categories of Feelings

Levels of Intensity	Happy	Sad	Angry	Scared	Confused	Strong	Weak
High	Excited Elated Overjoyed	Hopeless Sorrowful Depressed	Furious Seething Enraged	Fearful Panicky Afraid	Bewildered Trapped Troubled	Potent Super Powerful	Overwhelmed Impotent Small
Medium	Cheerful Up Good	Upset Distressed Down	Annoyed Frustrated Agitated	Threatened Insecure Uneasy	Disorganized Mixed-Up Foggy	Energetic Confident Capable	Incapable Helpless Insecure
Low	Glad Content Satisfied	Sorry Lost Bad	Uptight Dismayed Put Out	Timid Unsure Nervous	Bothered Uncomfortable Undecided	Sure Secure Durable	Shaky Unsure Soft

...So That You can Encourage Helpee Exploration

Perhaps you have had some difficulty coming up with feeling words that are interchangeable with Tom's feelings. Remember, always return to your observations for explicit cues to an actual helpee's feelings.

If you can't find the *"right"* word but you know you're in the *"ball park,"* try this technique. Ask yourself *"When I feel _____(general feeling)_____, how do I feel?"* For instance, if the helpee says *"I feel helpless"* and you find yourself at a loss for a new word to respond with, ask yourself *"How do I feel when I feel helpless?"* You might answer *"stuck."* **Look** at the helpee—does the helpee feel stuck? If not, repeat the question—only this time use *"stuck"* as the stimulus. *"How do I feel if I feel 'stuck?'"* You might say *"I feel down."* Continue to recycle the question and check out the new feeling words with your observations of the helpee until you have an interchangeable feeling word.

How do I feel
when I feel _____?
(general feeling)

Checking Out Your Feeling Words

RESPONDING TO FEELINGS AND CONTENT

Responding separately to the feeling or the content of the helpee's expression is not enough. Our response must be enriched by putting the feeling together with the content for the helpee.

Content is used to make the feeling meaningful. The content gives the intellectual meaning to the helpee's expression of her experience. The feeling gives the emotional meaning to the helpee's expression of her experience.

Responding to Feeling and Content

Remember, feelings are about content. For example, let us look at several feeling states and the related content areas:

Feeling	Content
Happy	about being promoted
Angry	toward my teacher for giving me a low grade
Sad	when I knew that I'd never see her again

You may practice supplying the content of different feeling responses in your own life as well as others.

Feelings About Content

In complementing a feeling response with a content response, we are usually providing the reason for the feeling. This type of response serves to help us understand more fully why the person feels the way she does. Content helps to clarify the basis for the feelings for both helper and helpee.

Content puts the feeling in context. The context is the helpee's relationship with other persons and her world in general. Understanding the context facilitates later phases of helping in which the helpee moves to act upon her world.

Why does he feel that way?

Providing a Reason for the Feeling

A response is not complete until it communicates both feeling and content. A helpful response complements feeling with content. Understanding of the helpee's expression can be communicated by complementing a response to feeling with a response to content. For example, whereas *"You're saying that _____"* expressed the content of the helpee's expression and *"You feel _____"* expressed the helpee's feelings, *"You feel _____ because _____"* captures both the feeling and the content. This is an effective format for a complete **interchangeable response** to the helpee.

You feel _____
because _____

Responding Interchangeably

It is as if we try to understand with our minds what a person feels in her gut. We do this first by crawling inside of her feeling. We do this second by comprehending the content of her expression.

Whereas *"You feel sad"* expressed the helpee's feelings with the passing of a loved one, *"You feel sad because she was the most important person in the world to you and now she is gone"* captures both the feeling and the content.

You feel sad because
she is gone.

Capturing Both the Feeling and the Reason

If we do not respond to the content of the helpee's expression we will often find ourselves unable to work with her problem. Things that we can frame in our minds are easier to do something about than those which we feel only in our gut. If we do not respond to the content and the feeling, we will not be able to bring the helping process to an action stage. We will not be able to help to change the helpee's behavior. We will have failed her and she will fail herself.

Let us spend another moment with Tom. He is angry and states *"I am just so angry at them. First they give me the opportunity and then they take it away."* Formulate a response that reflects both the feeling and content expressed by Tom.

You feel furious because they cheated you out of a real chance.

Beginning to Work with the Problem

Sometimes the helpee expresses multiple feelings and contents. It is important for us to attend to all of the major feelings and contents.

Now Tom is saying a lot more than that he is angry. If your response to his initial expression was effective, he might add *"Now it's gone and I won't ever get it again."* Formulate a response that captures the feeling and content of his new expression.

You feel sad because the opportunity is lost.

Responding to Many Feelings and Contents

If you respond accurately to Tom's expressions, you will involve him in exploring himself in the areas in which he is having difficulty. Because you have understood him accurately at the level that he has presented himself, he will go on to share many other personal experiences of this and other situations.

He will also bring his friends around because you are a good helper. It is time to meet some of these friends.

One is Joan—a cautious young woman. As a young person growing into adulthood, she is increasingly aware of her uniqueness as a woman. And acutely aware of the differences in her experiences from young men. She is also increasingly aware of the conflicts arising out of her desires for a professional career.

While you attend to Joan, she is reserved. Although Tom is now comfortable with you, she looks you over carefully. You might formulate an effective response.

You feel unsure of me because
 I might not be able to
  understand you.

Responding to Difficult Feelings and Contents

There are as many responses as there are people. As helpers, we must learn to attend to all of these people and to break free of our own restrictive experiences to enter their worlds and individualize our responses.

Another of Tom's friends is Floyd — an expressive young man. Floyd is black. Just as being a woman makes a difference in experience, so does being a young black man. Floyd is assertive in expressing this: *"You can never know what it is like to be me!"* Formulate an effective response to Floyd's expression.

You feel skeptical that I can ever know what you experience.

Responding to Different Feelings and Contents

One way of structuring responding is to test the comprehensiveness and accuracy of your response to the helpee's expression. Simply attend, observe and listen to the next expression you hear. Rate your accuracy of responding to the helpee's experience as follows:

High responsiveness — Accurate interchangeable response to feeling and content

Moderate responsiveness — Accurate interchangeable response to feeling

Low responsiveness — Accurate interchangeable response to content

As can be seen, the low levels of responsiveness are consistent with the high levels of attentiveness (listening and repeating verbatim). The moderate levels of responsiveness involve responding to feeling while the high levels of responsiveness involve responding to both feeling and content.

I just can't get this stuff.

You feel down because . . .

Levels of Responding

Now you can continue to build upon your own cumulative rating scale for helping. If the helper is attentive and responsive to feeling and content, you can rate the helper at fully responsive levels (level 3.0). If the helper responds to feeling alone, you can rate the helper at partially responsive levels (level 2.5). If the helper is attending and responding to only the content of the helpee's expression, you can rate the helper at less than facilitative levels (level 2.0).

5.0
4.5
4.0
3.5
3.0 *Responding to feeling and content*
2.5 *Responding to feeling*
2.0 *Responding to content*
1.5 *Attending physically*
1.0 *Non-attending*

Levels of Helping: Attending and Responding

The important thing is not what words you employ but how you enter the helpee's frame of reference to understand the feeling and content which she has expressed. And how you communicate that understanding at the level that she has expressed her concerns.

Joan may acknowledge the possibility that you might help her but she is going to be cautious before involving herself. Floyd may acknowledge that you can help him but only if you acknowledge that there may be limits to the depth of your understanding.

Indeed, you may respond to each as part of a group. You may communicate to each your understanding of his or her frame of reference. You may also facilitate each person's understanding of the others' frames of reference.

You should continue to practice responding to other people whom you meet in your daily living. As you practice, your own skill level will increase and you will be better prepared to enter the frame of reference of others.

To learn this,
I have to apply
it in my life.

Practicing Attending and Responding

Again, the function of responding to the helpee's experience is to facilitate her self-exploration of areas of concern. The areas explored by the helpee should be accompanied by feelings that are appropriate to the material being explored. Our awareness of the goals of exploring feeling and content will enable us to reinforce those helpee behaviors that accomplish the goals.

When the helpee becomes able to explore herself at levels interchangeable with those she has expressed, she signals her readiness for the next goal of helping — understanding. As helpers, we understand that there is no value to exploration unless it facilitates an understanding that goes beyond the material presented. The helpee must explore where she is if she is to understand where she is in relation to where she wants to be. The helpee's readiness for understanding signals the helper to begin **personalizing.**

Preparing for Personalizing

personalizing

*As children mature to adolescence, we begin to under-
stand the variety and the richness of experiences that make
them truly unique. They are attempting to define themselves
in terms of who they are and who they want to be. They
need "something more."*

*Part of this "something more" that we offer them in-
volves our being able to go beyond their expressions — to be
able to put together pictures that will guide their understanding of themselves in relation to their world — to be
able to personalize their experience of where they are and
where they want to be.*

*We demonstrate our maturity by adding to the pictures
which they have of themselves and their world or by developing our own pictures where they are unable to do so. We
motivate them to want to achieve maturity by the accuracy
of the pictures which we share with them and by the utility
of these pictures for them in their daily lives.*

*By personalizing our adolescents' experiences, we come
to realize fully that each one of them is indeed an exceptional child.*

Personalizing

To be truly effective in helping, then, we must be able to go beyond the material which the helpee presents. We must, in a very real sense, be able to add to her expressions. In addition, we must be able to filter this new understanding through our experience and come up with our own direction in the helping situation.

When we add accurately to the material which the helpee has expressed, we are personalizing. **Personalized empathy simply attempts to enable the helpee to understand where she is in relation to where she wants or needs to be.**

Personalizing involves building a base of interchangeable responses before personalizing the meaning, the problem, the feelings and the goal.

If we cannot personalize in our understanding, we cannot bring the helping process to culmination. We cannot enable the helpee to go beyond the experiences that were over-whelming her in the first place.

I need to know what
all this adds up to for me.

Personalizing Facilitates Helpee Understanding

Before we proceed to learn personalizing skills, let us take stock of how you have experienced personalizing understanding in your life. Remember what we have learned about how we can show people that we understand by responding to where they are right now? What do you do to crawl into their experience and communicate your understanding of where they want to go?

You know from your own life that you do not always say what you mean, let alone understand the implications of it. Sometimes you do not know what the real problem is. How have people helped you to understand your real problem? How have they helped you to define goals? What did they say to you?

The answers to these questions lead directly to learning the personalizing skills that facilitate the helpee's understanding of where she is in relation to where she wants to be in helping.

Thinking About Personalizing

BUILDING A BASE FOR PERSONALIZING

In order to make personalized empathic responses, we must first **build a base of interchangeable responses.** This is perhaps the most important task in helping — building an accurate base of understanding. If we can build a solid base of understanding, helping is possible. A fully alive communicative process and the resolution of problems are possible only if we have built upon the necessary foundation of understanding. If we cannot create an accurate base of understanding, helping is not possible.

The first step is a solid base of understanding.

Responding ▶ Building a Base for Personalizing

The more interchangeable responses we make to the helpee's experience, the higher the probability that we will be accurate when we attempt to personalize her understanding of herself. It simply makes good sense that if we respond to each piece of her experience accurately we increase the chances of putting all of the pieces together. In addition, as we respond to each experience we find that we are becoming increasingly accurate with the presentation of each new experience.

That's exactly it.

Increasing Accuracy

The first goal in learning to understand the helpee at the deepest levels, then, will be to formulate at least six responses that are interchangeable with the feeling and content expressed by the helpee. This must be accomplished for a large number of helpee expressions. That is, we must respond to helpee expressions in an extended exchange. And we must do so in a way that captures the helpee's expressions at the level that she is presenting them.

Have we explored all
the content and feelings?

Extending the Responsive Base

One burning question that Tom has is about the value of college for him. He may make a series of expressions. Drawing upon the skills which you have learned, you can formulate an effective response to each of these expressions.

"I just don't know what I'm going to do. My parents want me to stay in school but I'm not sure."

"I'm not sure I ever wanted to do this in the first place."

"They say they only want what's best for me but they never seem to take me into consideration."

"They're all over me. Everything I do, they have something to say."

You feel resentful because they made decisions which you aren't sure are right.

Making Interchangeable Responses

Responding to the helpee at interchangeable levels in extended conversation ensures your understanding of each of her expressions at the level she is presenting it. If each of your responses incorporates both relevant feeling and content at the level that the helpee has presented herself, then you have formulated extended interchangeable responses.

When we offer the helpee interchangeable responses in an extended conversation, we say that we have established an *"interchangeable base of communication."* An interchangeable base of communication assures us of understanding the helpee for the widest possible range of expressions.

You feel smothered because there doesn't seem to be any room for you.

Establishing an Interchangeable
Base of Communication

Helpers, and especially helper-trainees, sometimes feel the need to ask questions. Perhaps the details of the situation seem unclear. Or the causes of the problem have not been mentioned. Or the helpee hasn't disclosed what solutions she has tried. Rather than succumb to the urge to ask questions, the skilled helper will pause and mentally review the behavioral and verbal cues the helpee exhibits. This intensified use of the basic attending, observing and listening skills will allow the helper to respond to the helpee and thus encourage her to explore more fully. For example, instead of asking, "How have you been?", the disciplined helper will observe the helpee's behavior and respond, "You look like things have been going well." Instead of inquiring, "What exactly did they do?", the helper could offer, "You seem upset by what they've done." Or instead of asking, "What have you tried to do?", the helper could say, "You feel down because you haven't been able to handle the situation." This responsive method of encouraging the helpee to explore more fully places the burden on the helper, where it should be, and tends to prevent the helpee from becoming defensive.

Any questions that are asked need to be good ones. The test of a good question is whether you can respond to the helpee's answer. The skilled helper will sandwich any question she asks between two interchangeable responses. Of course, if you find yourself asking two consecutive questions without responding, then, in all probability, you are asking bad questions and should return to using your basic responding skills exclusively.

Responding — Not Question Asking

Establishing an interchangeable base of communication works for both helper and helpee. It prepares the helpee for movement to deeper levels of understanding. It also prepares the helper for movement to deeper levels of understanding.

Perhaps most important, it gives each an opportunity to check the other out and assess her readiness for movement to personalized levels of understanding. Our helpees can determine if we are *"with"* them. We can determine if we are *"with"* our helpees. Moreover, we can determine if the helpee is ready for movement to deeper levels of understanding.

If we have responded effectively to Tom, he may go on expressing himself in ways to which we can respond.

"I know how I feel but somehow I just never got to tell them."

"They don't really seem to care how I feel."

"I'm not always sure myself how much I care, I guess."

"I guess if I felt strongly enough I'd do something about it."

"I just want to do what's right and it's not always clear to me."

You feel frustrated
because things have never
been clear enough to act on.

Preparing Helpee and Helper for Understanding

With each expression, the helpee is spelling out more and more of her experience and we are becoming more and more attuned to the helpee's experience. Each of our responses should have contributed to establishing a base that is interchangeable in terms of the feeling and content expressed by the helpee.

When we have established an interchangeable base of communication, we can move with confidence to personalized levels of understanding. The interchangeable base assures us of the highest probability of success in understanding the helpee at deeper levels.

You feel determined
because it's important
to find the right way.

Continuing to Respond Interchangeably

The helpee often informs us directly through her behavior of her readiness to move to the next stage of helping. She alerts us to her readiness by demonstrating her ability to sustain her self-exploratory behavior without our help. She alerts us to her readiness by demonstrating her ability to make responses that are interchangeable with her own earlier expressions. In other words, she informs us of her readiness for movement by doing for herself the things that we have been doing for her.

At the same time, she asks us to do *"more"* for her. She asks us to go beyond what she was first able to do with our help and now is able to do for herself. She asks us to go to personalized levels of understanding.

The helper is guided in her movement to each stage by what is effective for the helpee.

I feel strongly that
I want to go on.

Signaling a Readiness to Move On

PERSONALIZING THE MEANING

The most difficult aspect of the helping process involves going beyond the helpee. Yet the ability to go beyond what another person has expressed, to identify why her experiences are important and what it is about her that is causing the situation, is precisely what distinguishes the helper from the helpee. The helper can do this consistently and with accuracy. The helpee cannot do this. The helpee may attempt to go beyond the helper but she always falls short.

When we go beyond the helpee and understand the meaning of the situation and the helpee's personal deficits, we say that we are personalizing. Content only becomes **meaning**ful when it is personalized for the helpee. We are personalizing the helpee's experiencing of herself by facilitating her self-exploration, self-understanding and eventual action. When we personalize, the helpee will come to experience herself more accurately in the area of her concern. We do this by drawing increasingly upon our own experience.

Building a Base ▶ Personalizing Meaning

Personalizing the meaning is the first step toward helping the helpee to understand where she is in relation to where she wants to be. We personalize the meaning when we relate the meaning directly to the helpee's experience. In other words, we zero in on why the experience is significant for the helpee. Whereas in responding to feeling and content we answered the question *"What is the situation and how does the helpee feel about it?"*, now we answer the question *"What is the effect of the situation of the helpee?"* Another way of asking this question is to ask *"What are the implications for the helpee?"*

In responding to feeling and content we used the format *"You feel_____ because _____."* This was effective because we did not yet know the personal impact the situation had on the helpee. Now we are asking the helpee to personalize the meaning. We are asking the helpee to understand why the experience is important. We now use the format, *"You feel_____ because* **you**_____ _____.*"*

You feel_____
because you _____.

Personalizing Meaning

Let us practice personalizing meaning. We will attempt to formulate a response that internalizes the meaning. So often we find that the helpee is talking about what a third person — another student, a teacher, a spouse — has done. Yet, most often, we cannot do anything about the third party's behavior. We can only work directly with the helpee. Now we are going to formulate a response that captures the impact of the situation on the helpee. For example, Tom expressed his experience of his lost opportunity: *"I am just so angry at them. First they give me the opportunity and then they take it away."* We responded interchangeably to Tom's experience: *"You feel furious because they cheated you out of a real chance."* Now try to help Tom understand why the experience is significant for him. Use the format *"You feel_____ _____ because you_____."*

You feel furious because you
learned the hard way not to hesitate.

Identifying the Significance of the Experience

Personalized responses are always formulated from the helpee's frame of reference. They acknowledge the helpee's experience of the world and build upon that experience.

Just as we formulated a personalized meaning response to an individual helpee expression, we can also develop a personalized response to helpee expressions made over a period of time.

What we do is to look for the common themes in the helpee's expressions. The themes relate to what the helpee is saying **about herself.** Common themes are those which are interwoven through more than one of the helpee's expressions. There may be several common themes or there may be one common theme woven through all of the helpee's expressions.

Certain feelings about
yourself keep coming up.

Using the Common Themes

When one common theme stands out above the others, we call it a *"dominant"* theme. A theme may dominate because of its recurrence or it may dominate because of the intensity of the expressions attached to it. We will tend to reinforce the expression of those themes experienced most intensely by the helpee. Dominant themes stand out as the most significant of the common themes made by the helpee.

Again, common or dominant themes may occur at both feeling and personalized meaning levels; but they tend to emphasize the meaning which the helpee is expressing. That is, they tend to emphasize the helpee's personal experience in relation to the world.

One thing you experience personally
in relation to your world keeps
coming up over and over...

Developing the Dominant Theme

PERSONALIZING THE PROBLEM

The next step in adding to the helpee's understanding
of where she is in relation to where she wants to be is **personalizing the problem.** This is the most critical task of helping.
We personalize the problem when we help the helpee to
understand what she cannot do that has led to her experience.
We answer the question *"What is it about the helpee which is
contributing to the problem?"*

In responding to personalized meaning, we looked at the
impact of the situation on the helpee. Now we are asking the
helpee to take responsibility for her own life and look at how
she herself is contributing to the problem.

How is he
contributing to the problem?

Personalizing Meaning ▶ Personalizing Problems

In personalizing the problem, we will attempt to formulate a response that defines the helpee's deficit behaviors. In other words, we ask and answer the question, *"What does the helpee lack that led to this situation?"* The statement of the helpee deficit must be in concrete behavorial terms if it is to be effective. Use the format, *"You feel _____ because you cannot _____"*.

You feel_____
because you
can't _____.

Personalizing Problems

Let us practice personalizing the problem. Again, this is the most important task of helping. To continue our illustration, we have responded to Tom's experience of his lost opportunity by responding interchangeably and by personalizing the meaning. Now try to help Tom understand what it is that he lacks that contributed to his difficult experience. Be sure that you describe something that Tom can't do and not something someone else who is involved in the problem should do. Use the format *"You feel_____ because you cannot_____."*

You feel angry
because you can't act
immediately on an opportunity.

Identifying Helpee Deficits

Sometimes we facilitate identifying helpee deficits through confrontations. Confrontations may take many forms. We may confront the helpee with behavior that disagrees with what she says. Sometimes we point to a discrepancy between how she says she feels and how she looks. Other times between how the helpee really is and how she wants to be. Or between insight and action. Also, we may confront strengths as well as weaknesses. In making our confrontations, it is usually most effective to use the format for a mild confrontation: *"On the one hand you say/feel/do* _____ *and on the other hand you say/feel/do* _____ *."* When such confrontations are made in the context of a personalized relationship, they may serve to promote open-ended inquiries into the behaviors. Remember, confrontations are never necessary and never sufficient. However, in the hands of an effective helper, they may be efficient for the purposes of recycling further exploration and understanding.

On the one hand, you speak one way and on the other hand, you behave another.

Confronting Helpee Deficits

PERSONALIZING THE FEELING

The next step in helping the helpee to understand where she is in relation to where she wants to be is **personalizing the feeling.** Now that we have personalized the meaning and the problem, we need to check back to see whether we have used the proper feeling response. In other words, we are going to ask and answer these questions: *"What are the implications of the personalized meaning and problem for the feeling? Does our new-found problem change the helpee's feeling?"* In particular, we are asking and answering the question *"How does the fact that the helpee has this deficit make her feel about herself?"* Personalizing the feeling is really an extension of personalizing the problem. Clearly, personalizing the feeling is predicated upon accurately personalizing the problem.

How does she
feel now?

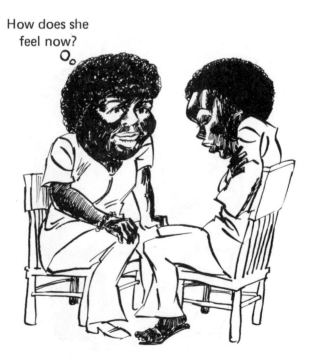

Personalizing Problems Personalizing Feelings

Most helping processes involve responding to self-disappointment. In other words, the helpee is usually disappointed in herself because she lacks the responses to handle the situation.

Let us practice personalizing the feeling. We will attempt to formulate a feeling response to Tom that is appropriate to our personalized meaning and problem response. Ask *"How does the newly personalized problem change the response to Tom's feelings?"* Try to communicate a more accurate understanding of the feelings he has inside or his feelings toward himself. Use the same format that you employed for personalizing the problem: *"You feel _____ because you cannot _____ ."*

You feel disappointed in yourself because you can't act immediately on an opportunity.

Personalizing Feelings

When we formulate a personalized response, we call upon our own experience to interpret the helpee's experience. It is as if we are filtering her experience through ours.

The personalized response that will make the most difference is the response to the personalized problem of the helpee. Personalizing the problem involves responding to behaviors that make the helpee vulnerable. Personalizing the feeling emphasizes how the helpee feels about these deficits. Understanding the helpee's deficits and her feelings about them will help the helpee to understand the goal.

Identifying Feelings About Deficits

PERSONALIZING THE GOAL

The final step in helping the helpee to understand where she is in relation to where she wants to be is **personalizing the goal.** We personalize the goal when we establish where the helpee wants to be in relation to where she is. One way to personalize the goal is to determine the behavior that is the opposite of the personalized problem. In other words, the goal behavior is defined as the *"flip side"* of the problem behavior. Goals or desired assets are determined by problems or present deficits. In personalizing the goal, we now use the format, *"You feel _____ because you cannot _____ and you want to _____."*

    You feel _____
because you cannot _____
  and you want to _____.

Personalizing Problems Personalizing Goals

Now let us practice personalizing the goal. We will attempt to formulate a response that defines the helpee's goal behaviors. In responding to Tom, we have personalized the feeling and the problem. Now we simply flip over the problem to determine the goal. We use the new format *"You feel _____ because you cannot _____ and you want to _____."*

You feel disappointed
because you can't act
immediately on opportunities
and you want to be able to.

Personalizing Goals

Formulating the response in such a way as to highlight and personalize the common or dominant themes of the helpee's expressions about herself facilitates the helpee's understanding of herself in relation to her world. The helpee is able to put her experience into perspective in a way that she was unable to prior to helping. Indeed, it is often the overwhelming nature of the problem that prevented her from getting a perspective and led her to seek help in the first place.

Returning for a moment to the earlier interaction with Tom, let's see if we can put the personalized understanding process together. Let us assume that Tom makes somewhat different responses to our responses.

Tom: "I'm just so angry with them. First they give me the opportunity and then they take it away."

Helper: "You feel furious because they cheated you out of a real chance."

Tom: "Now it's gone and I won't ever get it again."

Helper: "You feel sad because you may never get another chance as good."

Tom: "I'm just not able to get myself mobilized."

Helper: "You feel sad because you cannot say and do the things you need to get started."

Tom: "Worse than that, I rejected the opportunity like a big timer."

Helper: "You feel disgusted with yourself because you cannot act immediately when an opportunity comes along."

Tom: "What can I do?"

Developing the Personalized Goal

Your personalized understanding response should add to the helpee's level of self-understanding. It should put together the pieces of experience related by the helpee into a picture that the helpee can work with. She should be able to understand where she is in relation to where she wants to be. The ultimate test is a functional one. Either the helpee can work with your response or she cannot. Either the response enables her to go on to deeper levels of self-exploration and self-understanding or it does not. That is why building the interchangeable base is so critical in preparing the helpee for the personalized responses.

You feel disgusted because you can't act immediately and you want to be able to do this.

Completing the Personalized Goal

Let us return again to Floyd as he works a problem through. Formulate interchangeable responses to each of Floyd's expressions. Then formulate a personalized response to meaning. Finally, formulate a response to a personalized problem, feeling and goal.

"I just don't know what I'm going to do. On one hand, I really want to go. On the other, I don't want to go."

"Sometimes I'd just like to delay and not decide at all."

"I guess I just can't make decisions."

"I guess I really can't fool myself any longer."

"I'm just going to have to grow up and suffer the consequences."

Practicing Personalizing the Goal

Formulating an effective personalized response is the key to helping. If you can enter the helpee's frame of reference and enable her to see things clearly, you will help her to take the major step in changing her behavior. If you cannot do so, she will not have the perspective necessary for developing a direction that leads out of her difficulty.

You can test the effectiveness of your personalized responses by role-playing with associates. The effectiveness of your formulations may be determined by how well the helpee utilizes your personalized attempts. You might role-play some of the exercises in this book, then role-play other kinds of experiences before attempting to use your skills in real helping situations.

Again, the key to formulating effective personalized responses is discipline. Discipline in building an interchange-able base. Discipline in using that base to search out the common or dominant themes.

As we move to personalized levels of responding we are, as we have seen, automatically introducing our own experience. That is, we are going beyond what the helpee has expressed. In order to do this, we must be drawing from our own experience.

You feel fed up with yourself
because you cannot make decisions
and even though the price is high,
you want to learn to make them.

Personalizing Understanding

One way of structuring personalizing is to test the comprehensiveness and accuracy of your personalized response to the helpee's expression. Simply attend and respond in your next encounter. Then attempt to rate the accuracy of your personalizing the helpee's experience as follows:

    High personalizing — Accurately personalized problem, feelings and goal incorporating helpee's response deficit and helpee's response goal

    Moderate personalizing — Accurately personalized meaning incorporating personal implications of experience

    Low personalizing — Accurate responsiveness

As can be seen, the low levels of personalizing are consistent with the high levels of responsiveness (feeling and content). The moderate levels of personalizing involve meaning while the high levels involve the problem, feelings and goal.

You're scared because you might fail the course and you want to pass it.

. . . and I can't afford to flunk!

Levels of Personalizing

You can continue now to build your cumulative scale for helping. If the helper is attending, responding and personalizing the problem, feelings and goal for the helpee, you can rate the helper at fully personalizing levels (level 4.0). If the helper is attentive and responsive and personalizes the meaning for the helpee, you can rate the helper at facilitatively personalizing levels (level 3.5).

5.0

4.5

4.0 Personalizing problem, feelings and goal

3.5 Personalizing meaning

3.0 Responding to feeling and content

2.5 Responding to feeling

2.0 Responding to content

1.5 Attending physically

1.0 Non-attending

Levels of Helping: Attending, Responding, Personalizing

The function of moving to personalized responses, then, is to facilitate helpee self-understanding in the areas of concern to her. The helpee must understand where she is in relation to where she wants or needs to be. When the helpee comes to understand herself at personalized levels, she signals her readiness for using the next skill of helping—**initiating.** Initiating facilitates action and the helpee must act to get from where she is to where she wants to be.

At the deepest levels, we understand the helpee's need to act upon her understanding. Indeed, at the deepest levels there is no understanding without action.

Preparing for Initiating

5

initiating

Finally, our adolescents reach toward adulthood. They search out models for adult behavior. They try them out to see if they fit and modify them to meet their needs.

We are the models for adult behavior. If we have and can teach the skills that our youth need to live effectively in their worlds, they will incorporate these skills in their lives. In so doing, they embrace us and the way we live. If we don't have what it takes, our youth will reject our efforts because they cannot use them. In so doing, they reject us and the way we live.

When we act effectively to achieve goals in our own lives, we give our youth the model for adult behavior. When we initiate to help our children achieve goals in their lives, we are both model and agent for their growth to adulthood.

The final helpee goal, then, is **action.** Action involves a tangible change or gain in the helpee's behavior. In order to facilitate action, we initiate. Initiating involves operationalizing goals and initiating steps, schedules and reinforcements to achieve these goals.

Initiating means finding direction in life. Initiating means acting in following this direction. Initiating means bringing direction to culmination — giving life meaning in productivity and creativity.

Initiating

Before we go on to learn initiating skills, let us take stock of how you have experienced initiating action in your life. Hopefully, you are now moving into an area where you do very well. Usually we act. But often we do not have the understanding that personalizing skills help us to achieve.

Now that you understand someone, how detailed are the directions or actions which you have developed with them? Or, conversely, how detailed are the action steps which have been developed with you? Have you ever thought that you really understood what you needed to do, but when you went to implement it, you realized that you really did not have a plan? And it did not work! Many times as a helper you will find that you understand a problem and develop steps to solve it, but the helpees cannot follow the plan. Why is that?

The answers to these questions lead directly to learning the initiating skills that facilitate the helpee's acting to get from where she is to where she wants to be.

What can I
do about it?

Initiating Facilitates Helpee Action

INITIATING AN OPERATIONALIZED GOAL

If your helpee can identify with you as a helper, she opens herself up further to being influenced by you. You have seen the world through her eyes, filtered her perceptions through your own and attempted to make some sense out of the product. You must now attempt to develop some direction—however tentative. You must develop and operationalize the goals and the courses of action needed to achieve these goals.

Developing directionality is the crucial last phase of helping. The key to directionality is the disciplined manner in which you developed the helping process. If you have attended, responded and personalized with the helpee in a disciplined way, the different possible directions for the helpee will emerge more and more clearly.

You, the helper, are the key. You are the model. You enter helping with direction. You bring helping to its culmination—direction for the helpee. You will facilitate the helpee's search for direction to the degree that you are constantly searching out new directions for yourself. You will operationalize the helpee's goal to the degree that you can answer the question: *"How will we know when the helpee has reached the goal?"*

How will we know
when you have
reached the goal?

Personalizing Goals ▶ Operationalizing Goals

The new direction must be implemented in an action program. Defining or **operationalizing the helpee's goal** is the first step in developing an action program. Defining the helpee's operationalized goal is based upon the helpee's personalized goal. It is necessary to define the helpee's operationalized goal in terms that are observable and measurable. Defining a goal in observable and measurable terms usually means describing the goal in terms of the number of times, percent of time or amount of time the helpee will spend doing some behavior. Operationalizing will aid us in determining whether we achieved our goal or not. In personalizing the goal, we used the format *"You feel _____ because you cannot _____ and you want to _____."* Now in operationalizing the goal, we employ the format *"You want to ____(personalized goal)____ as indicated by ___(operational definition of the personalized goal)___ ."* In other words, we are answering the question *"How will we be able to tell when the helpee has reached the goal?"*

You want to _____
as indicated by
_____.

Operationalizing Goals

Let us practice operationalizing the helpee's goal. We will attempt to formulate a response that defines the goal in terms of the helpee's behaviors. For example, in responding to Tom's lost opportunity, we have defined his personalized goal as wanting *"to be able to act on presented opportunities."* In defining or operationalizing Tom's goal, we use the new format *"You want to_____as indicated by_____ _____."* For example, *"You want to be able to act on opportunities as indicated by the percent of times you set a goal and achieve it when you get the opportunity to do so."*

You want to be
able to....

Practicing Operationalizing the Goal

INITIATING STEPS TO THE GOAL

Simply defining the goal is not enough. To make a full delivery to our helpees, we also have to **develop steps** that outline how the helpee will reach the goal. A minimal action program should consist of the goal, a simple first step and an intermediary step halfway between the goal and the first step.

Developing the first step toward the goal is thus the second step in developing an action program. Developing the first step is based upon defining the goal. In other words, now that we have operationalized the helpee's goal we can develop the first step in a program to get her there. The first step is the simplest step that the helpee can take toward her goal. In developing the first step, we use the format *"Your first step is _____."*

Your first step
is _____ .

Operationalizing Goals  Initiating Steps

Let us practice developing the first step in an action program. We will attempt to develop a first step that leads the helpee toward her goal. For example, if the goal is running a mile the first step might simply be taking that first step.

For Tom, the first step must be based upon his need to develop goal-setting skills. Before he can develop goal-setting skills, he must conquer attending skills. Before he can set goals with regard to any matter, he must attend to, observe and listen to the material which he would use to identify the opportunity and set his goal.

Your first step is to pay attention to the world around you.

Initiating the First Step

The third step in developing an action program to achieve the helpee's goal is to develop intermediary steps to the goal. Intermediary steps bridge the gap between the first step and the goal. In other words, now that we have operationalized the helpee's goal and given her the first step to get there, we must develop intermediary steps to the goal. The intermediary steps will provide the necessary details to achieve the goal. They will ensure that the helpee gets to her goal.

Initiating Intermediary Steps

Let us practice developing the intermediary steps in an action program. We will attempt to develop the steps that lead the helpee from her first step to her goal. For example, if the goal is running a mile, the intermediary step might be to walk a mile or to run one-half mile.

For Tom, the first step toward goal-setting is paying attention. An intermediary step between paying attention and goal-setting is for Tom to learn to respond accurately to the world around him—just as you, the reader, have learned in this book to respond to the people around you. You would then work with Tom to develop additional intermediary steps that would ensure there are no gaps large enough to cause the failure of his program.

The process of developing an action program is the process of systematically building success into our lives. For example, one intermediary step between paying attention and responding would be observing. What would be some other intermediary steps?

Your intermediary step is to learn to respond to the world around you.

Developing Steps

INITIATING A SCHEDULE

Developing a course of action and steps to take along that course of action is not enough. The helpees with whom you work must act on the understanding and steps which have been developed. For it is only by action that real change and real growth can take place. Thus, as a helper you will want to do everything you can to make sure that your helpees act on the direction which you both have developed.

When can you start and finish each step?

Initiating Steps Initiating Schedules

The first step in implementation is **developing a schedule.** Specific start dates and completion dates must be developed for each action step. Time lines like this ensure that both the helper and helpee know not only what is to be done but also when it is to be done. This level of specificity helps to further define the goal. The more carefully the goal is defined, the more accurately its accomplishment can be evaluated.

Initiating Schedules

Tom decided that he would spend the next week learning and practicing to pay attention. The week after that he would work on developing his responding skills and the two weeks after that he would learn and practice goal-setting.

You can start tomorrow and finish 4 weeks from now.

Practicing Initiating Schedules

157

INITIATING REINFORCEMENTS

The final step in implementation involves **developing positive and negative reinforcers** that will encourage the helpee to take the needed steps. We are shaped most effectively when the consequences of our actions are immediate. The consequences of carrying out the steps to overcome the deficit are often too distant for the helpee. Such consequences lose their reality. Therefore more immediate reinforcers must be introduced. Like everything else in helping, the positive and negative reinforcers must be positive and negative from the helpee's frame of reference. We all know the story of the small child who fussed to get attention—because even negative attention was more positive than no attention at all.

How can we
ensure success?

Initiating Schedules ▶ Initiating Reinforcements

Tom decided that, as he completed each step in his program, he would allow himself to go out with his friends Friday and Saturday nights. If he did not complete the task, he would force himself to stay home and work on the step in his program during the evening hours.

Together, then, the steps of scheduling and reinforcement help to ensure that the steps in the program are taken. You, the reader, should develop your own schedule for implementing the steps in this book. You should also develop differential reinforcements to cover your positive and negative actions in taking the scheduled steps.

As you complete each step, you can _____.

Initiating Reinforcements

At the highest level of initiative, you as the helper may learn to use yourself as a potent reinforcer. You can do this by becoming conditional in your relationship. Conditionality means simply that the helper's behavior is contingent upon the helpee's behavior. You began in helping being unconditional in your regard. This unconditionality facilitated helpee exploration. You continued by communicating positive regard for the helpee's growth efforts. This facilitated helpee understanding. Now you may become conditional in order to facilitate helpee acting. Basically, what we do in being conditional with another person is to spell out the implications of their behavior for ours. In so doing, we put ourselves *"on the line."* We may use the simple format: *"If you say/feel/do_____ _____ then I will say/feel/do _____."* In communicating conditionality it is as if we are aligning ourselves with what is healthy in our helpees and in opposition to what is not healthy. It is as if we communicate our value for the person but not for her unhealthy behavior.

If you complete this step, then I will work with you on the next step.

Initiating Conditionality

One way of structuring initiating is to test the comprehensiveness of your initiative response to the helpee's experience. Simply attend, respond and personalize in your next encounter. Then attempt to rate the effectiveness of your initiative response to the helpee's experience as follows:

High initiative — Operationalization of steps
Moderate initiative — Operationalization of goal
Low initiative — Personalization of goal

As can be seen, the low levels of initiative are consistent with the high levels of personalizing (goal). The moderate levels of initiative involve operationalizing the goal while the high levels involve operationalizing the steps to achieve the goal.

Levels of Initiative

You can now complete your cumulative scale for helping. If the helper is attending, responding, personalizing and initiating the steps to achieve the operational goal, then the helper is operating at fully initiative levels (level 5.0). If the helper is initiating only to operationalize the goal, then the helper can be rated at facilitatively initiative levels (level 4.5).

5.0 Initiating steps

4.5 Initiating goal operationalization

4.0 Personalizing problem, feelings and goal

3.5 Personalizing meaning

3.0 Responding to feeling and content

2.5 Responding to feeling

2.0 Responding to content

1.5 Attending physically

1.0 Non-attending

Levels of Helping: Attending, Responding, Personalizing, Initiating

Now let's practice our own skills in a sample interaction—and see how an effective helper might respond. Tom and Floyd have been getting into an increasing number of arguments lately. They seem to have trouble seeing others—and being seen themselves—as uniquely worthwhile individuals.

Let's see if you can
formulate effective
responses to Floyd and Tom.

Practicing Helping

In the extended interaction that follows this page, you might use a piece of paper to cover the helper responses while you practice formulating your own responses to Tom and Floyd.

After you have made your best responses to Tom and Floyd, you might slide the piece of paper down and compare your responses to those of the helper.

Formulating Responses to Tom and Floyd

Helpee Involving/Helper Attending	Type of Response

Floyd: *"Man, I don't see how this jive is gonna get us anywhere!"*

Helper: *"It's pretty frustrating to try working these things through without anyone's help. If you're free the next hour, I'd like to get together with you in my office."* **Informing**

Tom: *"It's O.K. with me, I guess."*

Helper: *"What about you, Floyd? I'd like to spend a little time getting to know both of you better. Then I'll be able to be more helpful."* **Encouraging**

Floyd: *"That's cool. What about a cup of coffee instead?"*

Helper: *"Coffee's fine. I can really learn as much right here as in my office."* **Attending Contextually**

Floyd: *"What do you want to learn about us?"*

Tom: *"Yeah. I mean, I know you've been checking us out for quite a while."*

Helper: *"So you've been using your observing skills, too. You've noticed that I've really been paying attention to you."* **Attending Personally**

Tom: *"Uh huh. What have you been — you know — learning from us?"*

Helper: *"Well, I see two young guys who care enough about each other to stay in there fighting with each other. One's maybe more worn out than he should be and the other one's kind of edgy."* **Observing**

Floyd: *"I can dig it! You've really been using your eyes to see us huh?"*

Helper: *". . . And my ears to hear, too."* **Listening**

Helpee Exploring/Helper Responding	Type of Response

Floyd: *"The thing that really hassles me is the way you all act like everything's cool and I'm just supposed to relax and keep smiling!"*

Helper: *"You're saying it really gets to you when whites seem to want you to lay back and accept things."* — **Responding to Content**

Tom: *"Man, we're all in this thing together! What's so special about you?"*

Helper: *"You don't see why Floyd has to make a special case out of himself."* — **Responding to Content**

Floyd: *"You don't see it, huh Tom? Well maybe if you woke up black one morning a lot of things'd come clearer to you!"*

Helper: *"You feel really angry."* — **Responding to Feeling**

Floyd: *"Yeah, right! I mean, no white person can know what it's like to be black."*

Helper: *"You feel really furious when someone who isn't black tries to tell you how to act."* — **Responding to Feeling & Content**

Tom: *"You got a lot of nerve to come on like that to me, man!"*

Helper: *"It makes you angry when Floyd doesn't seem to appreciate the way you act with him."* — **Responding to Feeling & Content**

Floyd: *"Listen you get treated like an individual. But me — either I get turned down flat, or else everyone wants to get alongside of my blackness without ever checking out who I really am on the inside."*

Helper: *"It burns you up that people never seem to get past your skin to what's underneath."* — **Responding to Feeling & Content**

Floyd: *"Damn straight! I could be a genius or a flat-out fool and it still wouldn't matter as much as the fact that I'm black!"*

Helper: *"It drives you wild because people just see how you look without ever caring what you do or how you feel.*
Responding to Feeling & Content

Tom: *"Listen, you're doing the same thing when you lump me in with every other white!"*

Helper: *"You feel angry and frustrated because Floyd doesn't see the ways you try to relate to him as an individual."* **Responding to Feeling & Content**

Floyd: *"It's not the same thing, man. It's not like being black."*

Helpee Understanding/Helper Personalizing   **Type of Response**

Floyd: *"Dig it! They don't know who I am and they really aren't open to finding out."*

Helper: *"It really gets you down because you're not seen as a real person."*   **Personalizing Meaning**

Tom: *"I'm trying — I really am but for him I'm just another 'whitey.'"*

Helper: *"You're frustrated because you're just another white."*   **Personalizing Meaning**

Floyd: *"Listen! It's a real drag — like having to run 10 miles just to warm up for a 100-yard dash. Like — well, take writing, for one. I tried to get on the board at the Lit. Magazine. But once they found out I wasn't into writing heavy race-type stuff, they weren't interested."*

Helper: *"It's infuriating because you can't find a way to get people to treat you like an individual in your own right."*   **Personalizing Problems**

Tom: *"I feel the same way man. If I could just convince you I really do see you as a person and not just a black."*

Helper: *"Tom, you get bummed out because you don't feel like a real person when Floyd sees you as just another white."*

        Personalizing Problems

Floyd: *"If I could just get through to people."*

Helper: *"You feel helpless because you can't get other people — especially Tom — to see you the way you really are."*

        Personalizing Feelings

Tom: *"In a way I'm in the same boat. Maybe I don't feel it as strongly as if I were black but it seems like the same thing to me."*

Helper: *"You feel like you're in the same boat — discouraged because you can't get the real you across to Floyd."*

        Personalizing Feelings

Floyd: *"I've got a lot to offer. I mean really, I'm into a lot of good things I'd like to share. Like — well, like my writing."*

Helper: *"Floyd, you feel miserable because you can't get other people to see what you really have to offer and you want to very badly."*

        Personalizing Goals

Tom: *"Listen, Floyd, there's nothing I'd like more than for you and me to get beyond this lame race stuff. I'd like for you to trust me and share with me."*

Helper: *"And Tom, you feel pretty low because you can't get Floyd to understand you and you really want to get him to see beyond your whiteness."*

        Personalizing Goals

Helpee Acting/Helper Initiating	Type of Response

Helper: *"So Floyd, you want other people to see you as an individual. And Tom, you want Floyd to see you as an individual. How could you each tell if you were reaching those goals?"*

                          Operationalizing the Goals

Floyd: *"A good indication for me would be if I could get on the board of the literary magazine without having to be the 'racial reporter.' "*

Tom: *"I'd just like to get rid of all my behaviors that Floyd feels are racist, so we can get beyond the color of our skins."*

Helper: *"O.K. Those sound like pretty realistic goals. Floyd, your first step might be to make a list of the real contributions you feel you could make to the magazine's operation. And Tom, your first step might be to ask Floyd what the things are that you do which he feels are basically racist."*

                          Initiating First Step

Floyd: *"Huh! That sounds O.K."*

Tom: *"Hey, I'm ready if you are."*

Helper: *"Tom, your next step could be to work with Floyd to prioritize which particular behaviors you should try to eliminate first. And Floyd, yours could be to find out what specific things a person has to be do be elected to the board."*

                      Initiating Intermediate Steps

Tom: *"I got you."*

Floyd: *"Yeah, you're making a whole lot of sense."*

Helper: *"When do you think you could be done with these beginning steps?"*

                          Initiating Schedules

Floyd: *"I can be done in a day or two."*

Tom: *"If Floyd has time, I could work on it tonight and tomorrow night."*

Helper: *"O.K. You might also decide to reward yourself for completing a step by doing something you really enjoy doing — but decide not to do it if you fail to take the step."*   **Initiating Reinforcements**

Floyd: *"That's O.K. with me."*

Floyd: *"Wow, the way you lay it all out it seems so easy! I can handle that for sure!"*

Helper: *"You feel a lot more hopeful because you begin to see how you can actually get where you want to go."*   **Responding to Feeling & Content**

In this brief exchange, a first directionful step was developed. It was developed by responding to Floyd and Tom individually and then interrelating their expressions until the tentative direction emerged. Obviously, this is only the beginning. There is more to do. Much more. And with an extended relationship, there will be other areas of concern.

Each direction is, of course, to be modified by the feedback from acting upon the direction. The feedback recycles a new phase of exploration, understanding and action for each individual.

Check yourself out. If you found that you could respond and initiate effectively, you are well on your way to becoming a helper. If you did not, reread the earlier sections of the book. The art of helping is not at all an easy skill to conquer.

We have a
lot more to do.

Recycling Phases

Sometimes, the direction is one that emerges more clearly for the helper than for the helpee. Sometimes, it involves the denial of certain directions. Always it involves the decisions for growth. Immediate growth. Long-term growth.

An illustration of these principles occurred in the relationship between Joan and Tom. They have been seeing each other for some time and have become increasingly intimate in a number of ways. One step which they still hesitate to take involves actually living together.

Again, practice your own responses to the expressions before checking out the effective helper's responses.

Let's try to help
Tom and Joan.

Practice Learning

Helpee Involving/Helper Attending	Type of Response

Helper: *"Hey, how about stopping by my office this afternoon about 2:00 and we can talk more about this."* — Informing

Joan: *"Yeah — that would be O.K."*

Tom: *"Sure, why not."*

Helper: *"Bouncing things off someone else can sometimes really help you get a clearer picture."* — Encouraging

Joan: *"O.K."*

Tom: *"See you later."*

That Afternoon

Joan: *"Your office is really nice."*

Helper: *"There are some things in here that students have given me that mean a lot to me."* — Attending Contextually

Tom: *"Yeah — it's almost like it's not an office at all. You really feel relaxed here."*

Joan: *"You look like you're ready to listen but it's kind of hard to get started."*

Helper: (Helper has seated herself directly opposite the couple and is leaning slightly toward them with good eye contact.) — Attending Personally

"You look a little hesitant too, Tom." — Observing

Tom: *"Yeah, I guess I am. At least you seem like somebody who really wants to hear what's on our minds."*

Helper: *"Yeah. Listening's a pretty important thing."* — Listening

Helpee Exploring/Helper Responding	Type of Response

Tom: *"Listening. Huh! I just wish my parents could get into some listening instead of just yelling at me all the time."*

Helper:	*"You're saying that your parents holler a lot and don't pay much attention to what you have to say."*	Responding to Content
Joan:	*"His parents and mine, too. Honestly, they treat us like we were little kids!"*	
Helper:	*"You feel pretty angry with them."*	Responding to Feeling
Tom:	*"They're living in a dream world."*	
Helper:	*"It bugs you that they're so out of touch."*	Responding to Feeling & Content
Joan:	*"They don't even know that the real world today is a whole new thing!"*	
Helper:	*"You feel mad because they don't even know what's going on."*	Responding to Feeling & Content
Tom:	*"I just wish they'd let up on us."*	
Helper:	*"You really resent that they're always on your back."*	Responding to Feeling & Content
Joan:	*"We both do. See, we've been making some plans of our own. Only they won't believe that we're — I don't know — mature enough to handle things!"*	
Helper:	*"It's frustrating when you parents don't accept your capability."*	Responding to Feeling & Content
Tom:	*"You know it! I mean, all we want to do is live together. That's no big thing today, right? But they're such jerks, they think we're going to ruin our lives!"*	
Helper:	*"You feel furious because they won't let you make your own decisions."*	Responding to Feeling & Content
Joan:	*"Exactly! We've tried to be responsible with them, but it hasn't helped. I don't know how we're supposed to convince them that we're — well, practically adults!"*	

Helper:	*"What it comes down to is that you are both fed up with the fact that they want to keep you on a leash and you want to live your lives on your own terms and not theirs."*	Responding to Feeling & Content

	Helpee Understanding/Helper Personalizing	Type of Response
Tom:	*"It's really a messed-up situation any way you look at it."*	
Helper:	*"It's a lousy feeling because even though you're pretty mad at your parents you still care a lot about how they feel."*	Personalizing Meaning
Joan:	*"I — yeah, I've thought about that."*	
Tom:	*"You have? About whether they might be right?"*	
Joan:	*"Yes."*	
Tom:	*"Well, I guess I've probably had some questions myself. I mean, how could we help it when our parents are making us look at the bad side all the time?"*	
Helper:	*"So you're kind of uneasy, too, Tom, because you're not confident enough in yourself to be sure you are doing the right thing."*	Personalizing Meaning
Joan:	*"It's like — well, when my parents tell me what to do, it makes me very defensive. But when I'm alone — I don't know — what if we went ahead and then found out we were making a mistake?"*	
Helper:	*"It concerns you because you can't figure out for sure what's the best thing for you both to do regardless of what others want you to do."*	Personalizing the Problem
Tom:	*"Uh huh. I mean — well, I love Joan too much to want to do something for the*	

> *wrong reasons — just to get back at my parents, for example."*

Helper: *"It's scary because you can't be sure you're doing the right thing for the right reasons."*   **Personalizing the Feeling**

Joan: *"That's just it. I — I don't think we would even be so ready to live together if our parents weren't so set against it."*

Helper: *"You feel kind of frightened because you can't stop living in reaction to your parents even though you want to make decisions that reflect who you are."*   **Personalizing the Goal**

Tom: *"Yeah, We've got to be ourselves."*

Helper: *"You're certain you want to be yourselves even though you're sometimes not sure what that really means."*   **Responding to Feeling & Content**

Helpee Acting/Helper Initiating   **Type of Response**

Helper: *"It sounds to me like your goal isn't really to live together — but that you really want to find a way to make decisions based on your own values, rather than just reacting to others. That really means being able to use your personal values to decide whether or not to live together."*

     Operationalizing the Goal

Tom: *"Yeah — but that's just it. Even when I know something is important, I can't seem to figure out what to do about it."*

Helper: *"It's confusing when you can't figure out how to live your own values. The first thing you might do is explore your values and then make a list of all the things that are important to you.*   **Initiating the First Step**

Joan: *"Sure — but how's that going to help us know what to do?"*

| Helper: | *"Well, once you know what's important, you can prioritize your values by deciding which one's most important, next important and so on — then you can use all this information to make the decision."* | **Intermediate Step** |

| Tom: | *"I get it — you mean some of our values ought to influence our decision more than others and we have to know that to make the best choice."* | |

| Helper: | *"That's right. When do you think you could make up a list of your values and priorities so we could get together again and talk them over."* | **Initiating Schedules** |

| Joan: | *"We can get that done this afternoon and tonight."* | |

| Helper: | *"O.K. If you do that, then I'll meet with you both again on Thursday to review what you've done and to show you how to use those values systematically to make the best choice for you."* | **Initiating Reinforcements** |

| Tom: | *"I think we're going to feel a whole lot better once we've worked this thing through."* | |

| Helper: | *"You already feel a lot better just knowing that you're going to be able to make the best decision based on the things that are really important to you."* | **Responding to Content & Feeling** |

It is as if in the helpee's darkness of indecision, the helper shares her light of directionality. She is an adult. She has learned from her experience. She does share her learning—indeed teach her learnings—to guide them through the difficulties and to help keep them from stumbling too much.

The helper enters their frames of reference and communicates her understanding. She also taps in on the very doubts which brought them to seek her out in the first place. In doing so, she uses her experience to help Joan and Tom develop their direction and yet she never needs to threaten or become arbitrary or judgmental.

Developing Directionality

While the helper shares the principles by which she lives, they are not binding upon the helpee. They simply represent potentially effective alternatives to the limited ways that the helpee has available. It is for the helpee to test them out in her experience and to make them her's—or not.

The growth process is one of expanding options and narrowing choices. Whether or not the helpee chooses to incorporate the helper's principles is not critical. What is critical is whether or not the helpee becomes involved in another cycle of learning—of exploration, of understanding, of action —that leads to her further growth.

Preparing for Helping

6

helping

Our adults have now reached full maturity. They can communicate fully with others. They have satisfied their needs for fullness in all aspects of their lives. They have become whole persons.

They are now prepared to help others to achieve their own levels of wholeness. They will not only communicate fully with others struggling to grow and develop. They will also teach the others the skills they need to grow and develop themselves. They will become both the models and the agents for the growth of others just as we have been for them.

They will give their lives meaning through their productivity in living, learning and working arenas. They will create new life through their helping skills.

The cycle of life continues.

Helping

APPLYING HELPING SKILLS

It is not so much what you do in the crisis as what you have done the other 364 days during the year. If you have attended to the helpee's needs and responded to her experience, you have facilitated her exploration of where she is. If you have personalized your understanding of the helpee, you have facilitated her understanding of where she is in relation to where she wants to be. And if you have initiated to help your helpee achieve her goals, you have facilitated her acting to get from where she is to where she wants to be. As you have developed the full helping process with the helpee, you have seen her solve her problems and achieve her goals. You have seen her grow and develop.

Helping Facilitates Exploration,
Understanding and Acting

But growth is not static. Growth is life-long learning. Learning is exploring, understanding and acting. Life-long learning involves recycling exploring, understanding and acting. When the helpee receives the feedback from acting, she can use it to stimulate more extensive exploring, more accurate understanding and more effective action. A growing person is constantly involved in the learning process in an ongoing, ever-expanding spiral of life.

Growing Recycles Exploration,
Understanding and Action

Growing is more than being helped. Growing is more than learning. Growing is helping others to learn. This means helping others to explore, understand and act. And then to recycle the learning process throughout life.

In this regard, there are a number of things that all people can do with each other in their daily contacts. First and foremost, each can begin by attending and making an effective response to the other.

Just as the effective counselor is constantly responding and initiating with the counselee, so will the counselee learn to respond and initiate with others.

Each parent can make at least one effective response to each other and each child each day. As the children grow, each child can learn to make an effective response to each parent and every other child each day. In a similar manner, each teacher or learner can learn to make an effective response to all other teachers and learners every week.

Growing Is Helping

Having begun by attending and responding, over an extended period of time, each person can learn to personalize and initiate with the people with whom they are involved. At the highest level of helping, people communicate with immediacy. Immediacy means understanding and interpreting in the moment what is going on between you and the helpee. Immediacy involves the highest levels of responsive and initiative behavior. It means living fully in the moment through responding fully to the helpee's experience and initiating fully from your own experience. It means being simultaneously aware of both the helpee's and your own experience.

Immediacy Is the Highest Level of Helping

A less-than-whole person is never actually talking about what she seems to be talking about. She is always talking about herself in relation or comparison to other people. While she may talk about third parties, the one person she is comparing herself with most is the person with whom she is talking. For example, Tom or Joan or Floyd may be talking about the difficulty he or she had in taking a school examination or a medical examination yet may really be telling us something about his or her feelings in the situation with us. The helper must be keenly aware that most of what the helpee is saying is being said in relation to the helper. That is, the helpee is rarely directly communicating what she is experiencing. In communicating immediacy that focuses upon the helpee's feelings, you may use the format: *"You feel _____ because I _____."* In essence, you are trying to understand the helpee's immediate feelings and content in relation to you.

You feel _____
because I _____.

Immediacy in Responding

A whole person is always talking about what she seems to be talking about. She is always communicating fully. One of our tasks as helpers is to become whole people. For helping is, in truth, a process of teaching people who do not communicate fully to communicate fully—with themselves and others. The effective ingredient in helping, then, is a whole person who communicates fully. In communicating with personal immediacy that focuses upon the helper's feelings, you may use the format *"I feel _____ because you _____ _____."*

I feel _____
because you _____.

Immediacy in Initiating

Whatever the effective helper or the whole person is doing, she is always checking back with the helpee. Whether she is initiating with the helpee to achieve a goal or communicating with immediacy, the helper is constantly checking out the accuracy of her response. She does this by making responses that are interchangeable with the feeling and content expressed by the helpee. This gives both helper and helpee the opportunity to check out the accuracy of the helper's response, no matter how advanced the stage of the helping relationship. Effective helpers are always checking up on the accuracy of their responses. Other people are never checking back.

You feel comfortable
with what I said.

Always Checking Back with the Helpee

Here is a final interaction involving Tom, Joan and Floyd. Their deeply-felt concerns about the world and their ability to live effectively in it are as profound as they are challenging. Try practicing your responses to the dialogue before checking these responses against those of the effective helper.

Let's practice our helping skills.

Putting It All Together

	Helpee Exploring/Helper Responding	Type of Response

Floyd: *"We're kind of angry with your whole generation. You left us all the mess — and the pollution and garbage."*

Helper: *"You're saying that we've copped out on the problems and stuck you with them."* — Responding to Content

Tom: *"Yeah, my parents, you, all of you people that have been around but haven't done anything to set things straight."*

Helper: *"It really makes you angry."* — Responding to Feeling

Joan: *"Yeah. And a lot of you did more than that — you sold out for bucks!"*

Helper: *"You feel furious that a lot of us settled for a messed-up world — for a price. I think a lot of us probably hung on to the idea that part of the 'price' would be a better world for our kids — for you."* — Responding to Feeling & Content

Floyd: *"Yeah, well maybe that's what you thought. But just look at the world you're getting ready to hand over to us."*

Helper: *"It's really frustrating for you because we sold out for the short-range view and missed out completely on the long-range conditions."* — Responding to Feeling & Content

Joan: *"You really blew it!"*

Helper: *"You really resent what we've done."* — Responding to Feeling & Content

Tom: *"Really! I mean, how are we supposed to act when the people who are supposed to know better act the way you all have?"*

Helper: *"You're sore because we're supposed to have the answers and yet it's pretty obvious we don't."* — Responding to Feeling & Content

Joan: *"Yeah, sure — only now it sounds like the whole load's on us!"*

Helper: *"It's frightening to have that responsibility dumped on you."*   **Responding to Feeling & Content**

Floyd: *"And it isn't fair!"*

Helper: *"You're really upset about being given the burden."*   **Responding to Feeling & Content**

          Helpee Understanding/Helper Personalizing   **Type of Response**

Tom: *"Right."*

Helper: *"And you feel resentful toward me for being part of it."*   **Immediacy**

Joan: *"Yeah, you're right. You are at fault, but I guess all we've done so far is make a lot of noise about what's wrong. We really haven't learned to do anything constructive about it yet."*

Helper: *"You feel a little foolish because you haven't shown you can handle it any better than we have."*   **Personalizing the Meaning**

Floyd: *"And if we can't?"*

Helper: *"That makes me feel responsible because you're really asking if I can give you any help right now. And if I can't, then the implications are pretty heavy for all of us."*   **Immediacy**

Tom: *"It really does make a difference, knowing we're not alone. I guess we still need a lot of help."*

Helper: *"And it's kind of frightening because you can't even figure out what it is you have to learn."*   **Personalizing the Problem**

Joan: *"Yeah, where do we begin?"*

Helper: *"You feel lost because you can't find a starting point."*   **Personalizing the Feeling**

Tom:	*"Yeah, but there's still time for us."*	
Floyd:	*"We haven't really had our chance yet."*	
Helper:	*"Uh huh — you feel good that you still have a chance to make things better, but it also makes you anxious because you don't know how to begin making things better and you really want to succeed."*	

Personalizing the Goal

	Helpee Acting/Helper Initiating	**Type of Response**
Joan:	*"We've got to succeed!"*	
Helper:	*"O.K. So the goal is to succeed where our generation has failed. What kind of things would indicate to you that you were succeeding?"*	Operationalizing
Tom:	*"If there was less pollution."*	
Floyd:	*"A fair chance for women, blacks and other minorities."*	
Joan:	*"If there was more honesty in government and business."*	
Helper:	*"Those are big problems. Which one is most important?"*	Operationalizing
Tom:	*"I think human rights has got to be number one."*	
Joan:	*"For sure."*	
Floyd:	*"Right. We ought to start right here with fair employment."*	
Helper:	*"So you would feel that you had made a successful start if over the next six months you could bring at least one major employer in the area into compliance with the equal employment opportunity guidelines."*	Operationalizing
Tom:	*"Great."*	

Floyd: *"I don't even know where to start."*

Helper: *"It's a big job. But one way you might*
begin would be to learn how to develop
an effective action — plan to get there."

                                      Initiating First Step

Joan: *"Right there we'd have to develop skills,*
wouldn't we? So we could really figure
out where we were going and how we
were going to get there."

Helper: *"That's right. And by getting planning*
skills, you'd be able to plan the other
skills you'd need to really attack the
problem. Your actual plan of attack
would represent another step."

                            Initiating Intermediate Steps

Floyd: *"Man, that'd be a whole lot better than*
just complaining and moaning and
wasting a lot of energy!"

Helper: *"It feels good to know you really can*
approach even the toughest problem
in a systematic way."   **Responding to Feeling & Content**

          "Another thing you can do is make sure
you work on at least one new skill each
week — and then figure out a system of
personal rewards and punishments de-
pending on whether you actually stay on
schedule."   **Initiating Schedules & Reinforcements**

Joan: *"I think you're trying to show us it really*
can be done — and I think I'm beginning
to believe you."

Helper: *"Things look a whole lot brighter when*
you begin to see that there is something
you can do to help!"   **Responding to Feeling & Content**

The helper working with Tom, Joan and Floyd is more than merely effective. She is fully alive, fully concerned—and fully capable of communicating her living energy, concern and capability to those who are most in need.

These three young people began—as many of us do—by focusing their critical intelligence everywhere but on themselves. In the end, however, they are able to see that such focus promotes only sterile revolution—not the dynamic evolution which stems from a fully alive, fully developed communicative process.

Helping Means Sharing Fully

In a fully alive communication process, each person may be helper to the other. But one must initiate the helping process by communicating her openness to understanding the other. In so doing, she establishes the model for the other to imitate.

A fully alive communication process means just that. A process in which each person attends to and responds fully with the other. A process in which each personalizes and initiates fully with the other. A process in which mutual problems may be solved.

It is what is represented in a good marriage and a healthy family. Each person can be fully herself or himself with the other and yet fully responsive to the other's fullness. Neither *"cops out"* on herself or the other.

Many of today's problems are related to this phenomenon of *"copping out."* There are an endless number of *"outs."* Drugs, including alcohol, are just one illustration of the easy ways in which people may choose to avoid dealing with the real issues for themselves. And the real issues involve whether people are willing to pay the price for functioning effectively or living fully.

Helping Means Not "Copping Out"

The price which people have to pay involves learning the skills which they need to know to live effectively in their worlds. Just as you learned to be a helper, you must also teach your helpees to be helpers. After attending, responding, personalizing and initiating with helpees, we must ultimately teach the helpees to attend, respond, personalize and initiate with each other. There is no *"edge"* in helping. The helping skills are transmitted to the helpees. The helpees are transformed to helpers.

Teaching Is the Preferred Mode of Helping

The helpee informs us that she is ready to function as a helper by her behavior. Not only can she formulate personalized responses to her own behavior but she can now sustain initiative in her life. She is capable of acting effectively and, perhaps more important, she is capable of modifying her behavior based upon the feedback which she receives from her action.

One clear demonstration of the helpee's readiness to terminate the helping process, to go out on her own, is her ability to respond to the experience of the helper. That is, whereas the helping relationship once revolved around the helpee's experience, she is now *"on top of things,"* has them in perspective and is able to respond accurately to the experience of others.

The clear demonstration of your ability to function as a helper will be your ability to respond and initiate effectively. If you cannot now do so with confidence, review the work again—particularly the beginning phases of helping, for they make the later phases possible. Search out the most effective of your peers and share the learning process with them.

> You feel pleased that
> you've been able to help us.

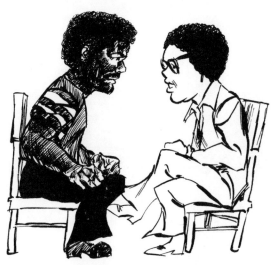

Mastering Helping Skills

HELPING SKILLS POST-TEST

If you have worked hard to learn and apply the skills in this book, you will want to take a moment now to reassess your level of helping skills.

Imagine that you have been interacting with the following client or helpee for about 30 minutes.

The helpee is a young father who has just been laid off from his job because the company he worked for moved its local offices to another part of the country. He says to you:

"Boy, I'm really in a bind. The bills are coming in and our savings are just about gone. I've got to find a job soon, but things are tight all over and nobody seems to be hiring."

On the following lines, write out what you would say
to this helpee. Try to communicate both understanding and
direction. Write the exact words you would use if you were
actually speaking to the helpee.

_____

_____

_____

_____

You probably felt more confident that you were making a helpful response than you did on the pre-test. Great! Your effort is paying off!

Now, before you assess your own response to this helpee, we will consider several alternative responses that might have been made by someone trying to help this person.

Next to each of the responses, you should write a number to indicate your rating of the effectiveness of that response. Use the following rating scale:

1—Very Ineffective
2—Ineffective
3—Minimally Effective
4—Very Effective
5—Extremely Effective

Rating Helper Responses

Your Ratings   **Helper Responses**

_____ 1. *"You feel frustrated because the bills are piling up and there just aren't any jobs."*

_____ 2. *"You feel that things are closing in on you and you've got to do something soon."*

_____ 3. *"Don't worry. You'll find a good job soon."*

_____ 4. *"You're really feeling scared because you don't know how to increase the odds of finding a job and you need work now.*

_____ 5. *"You're feeling desperate and really down on yourself because you can't find a job and you really need to get one soon. A first step might be for us to explore some job sources that don't usually advertise."*

Discriminating Helping Skills

You may be eager for some feedback about now. Check yourself out against the ratings of the trained raters. Response #3 was rated 1 because it was irrelevant to the helpee's expression and did not respond accurately to either the content or feelings expressed by the helpee.

Response #2 was rated 2 because it was an accurate response to the content of the helpee's statement but did not respond to the feelings expressed by the helpee.

Response #1 was rated 3 because it was an accurate response to both the content and the feelings expressed by the helpee. The response expressed an accurate understanding, of where the helpee is, but no direction. Response #4 was rated 4 because it was an accurate response to the personalized problem, feelings and goal expressed by the helpee and, therefore, conveyed understanding of both where the helpee is and where he wants to be. The response fell short of a 5 rating because it did not suggest a specific first step towards the helpee's goal.

Response #5 was rated 5 because it was an accurate response to the helpee's personalized problem, feelings and goal, and it also suggested a specific first step that the helpee could take toward the achievement of his goal. Thus this response provided both understanding of where the helpee is and where he wants to be and specific direction about how to get from where he is to where he wants to be.

Receiving Feedback

To calculate your post-test **discrimination** score, do the following things:

1. Without regard to whether the difference is positive or negative, write down the difference between each of your numerical ratings and each of the experts' numerical ratings.
2. Add up the difference scores. You should have five scores, one for each response alternative.
3. Divide the total of the difference scores by 5. The result is your post-test discrimination score.

Your post-test discrimination score should be better than your pre-test score. It should deviate one-half level or less from the expert ratings. If so, you should be quite pleased with yourself. If not, you will want to study the details of the feedback and return to reread those sections of the book where you had trouble.

RESPONSE	MY RATING	EXPERT RATING	DIFFERENCE SCORE
1	3 —	3	0
2	3 —	2	1
3	1 —	1	0
4	4 —	4	0
5	5 —	5	0

TOTAL 1

DIVIDE $5\overline{)1}$ = .2

POST-TEST DISCRIMINATION SCORE } = .2

Calculating

If you have mastered all of the helping skills in this book, you are now ready to rate your own responses, both on this post-test and on the pre-test at the beginning of the book. These ratings will indicate your **communication** scores, both before and after learning the skills of helping.

To rate your own responses, both now and in the future, you may wish to use the basic helping scale which follows. You will note that this scale is based on the specific skills which you have learned in **The Art of Helping.**

You can list these scores with your discrimination scores to complete your assessment of where you were and where you are now in terms of your helping skills. Your post-test communication score should be at least 3.0, and probably 4.0 or 5.0. If your score is less than 3.0, you will first want to carefully review the chapter on responding (Chapter 3). If your score is between 3.0 and 5.0, you will want to review the chapters on personalizing and initiating (Chapters 4 and 5) to learn how to develop better responses.

Pre-Test Communication Score_____

Post-Test Communication Score_____

Pre-Test Discrimination Score_____

Post-Test Discrimination Score_____

Assessing

Basic Helping Scale

5.0	Initiating steps
4.5	Initiating goal operationalization
4.0	Personalizing problem, feelings and goal
3.5	Personalizing meaning
3.0	Responding to feeling and content
2.5	Responding to feeling
2.0	Responding to content
1.5	Attending
1.0	Non-attending

Non-attending covers all behaviors, both verbal and non-verbal, that are unrelated or irrelevant to the helpee's situation or expressions.

Attending includes the verbal and nonverbal behaviors that are directly related to involving the helpee (e.g., attending physically), but do not respond to what the helpee has shared about where she is.

Responding to content involves summarizing what the helpee has shared concerning her situation.

Responding to feeling involves accurately identifying a feeling word that is interchangeable with the helpee's experience of the situation.

Responding to feeling and content involves the clear communication of helper understanding of both the content and feelings expressed by the helpee.

Personalizing meaning involves responding to identify the personal significance or implications of the expressed situation for the helpee.

Personalizing problem, feelings and goal involves responding to identify the personal deficits (or assets) of the helpee that are contributing to the problem or situation, the feelings that the helpee is experiencing about her deficits (or assets) and the goal that the helpee wants to achieve.

Initiating goal operationalization covers responses that express a clear understanding of the helpee's personalized problem, feelings and goal in behavioral terms.

Initiating steps involves responses that identify specific steps toward accomplishing the operationalized goal.

Each of the levels of helping skills above the nonattending level serves an important purpose in the helping process. Each helper behavior leads to an important helpee activity.

Attending leads to helpee **involvement**. Responding facilitates the helpee's **exploration**. Personalizing deepens the helpee's **understanding**. Initiating enables the helpee to **act** constructively.

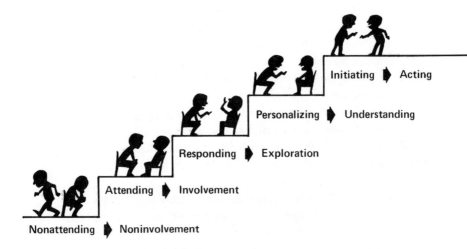

Initiating ▶ Acting

Personalizing ▶ Understanding

Responding ▶ Exploration

Attending ▶ Involvement

Nonattending ▶ Noninvolvement

Functions of Helping Skills

And, finally, each of the basic helpee activities—involvement, exploration, understanding and action—leads to new learnings and growth for the helpee.

Involvement leads to the helpee's reaching out and investing herself in the process of change. Exploration leads to a real clarification of where the helpee is in relation to her world and in relation to herself. Understanding leads to a full realization of where the helpee is in relation to where she wants to be. Action leads to the helpee's actually getting from where she is to where she wants to be. And action also produces the feedback necessary for a whole new cycle of learning—involvement, exploration, understanding and action. Thus, the cycle of growth is repeated.

I've learned a lot but
there's a lot more
I want to do.

Helping ▶ Learning

CONCLUSION

The secret to success in life involves three ingredients. The first of these is skills. In order to be effective in life we must be skilled.

We have learned the skills of helping. We must now go on to apply these skills with ourselves and others. As we apply them, we will recognize the need for more skills.

We will find that there are many other skills which we must learn. In so doing, we must learn the most basic of all skills: learning how to learn.

In addition, we will find that there are many skills which we must learn to teach others in order to help them fully. So we must also learn the basic skills of teaching.

Skills — The First Ingredient of Success in Helping

The second ingredient of success in life is discipline. In order to be effective in life we must employ our skills with discipline.

We have learned behaviors and formats for discriminating and communicating in helping. The precise behaviors and formats are not the effective ingredients. The accuracy of the discriminations and communications is the effective ingredient.

In the end, we will be guided by what is effective for the helpee. However, the behaviors and formats are effective indices which we may use to guide ourselves. If we use these skills in a disciplined way, we will know when we are deviating from the structure and functions of helping. For example, most fundamentally, the format, *"You feel _____"*, reminds us to use a feeling word to reflect the helpee's experience.

You feel . . .

Discipline — The Second Ingredient of Success in Helping

The third ingredient of success in life is work. Once we have learned the skills and employed them with discipline, we must work very hard.

Our real learning in life comes from our applying our skills with discipline in a variety of human experiences. In other words, our real learning in life comes from working very hard. Now, most professional helpers are overburdened with their caseloads. And most functional helpers are in demand for their skills. While they are working hard, they must also protect themselves by receiving the maximum return for the minimum investment. For example, they will tend to see people in small groups of eight to ten people as opposed to individual, one-to-one helping. Moreover, once they understand the response deficits of the helpees, they will tend to employ teaching in groups as the preferred mode of treatment.

Work — The Third Ingredient of Success in Helping

The point is this: our task in life is to improve the quantity and quality of human experience — our own as well as others.

Life is a process of development. Life is growth. And growth is learning new skills. Learning comes from working hard to apply the skills with discipline. The quantity and quality of our experience will be reflected in an expanded quantity and quality of responses; in a word, growth.

The effective ingredients of life are the same as the effective ingredients of helping. Understanding and action. Nourishment and direction. Responding and initiating. When we use these skills effectively, then we can be one healthy, happy family of humankind. Most importantly, we can help each other to actualize our human potential.

The only meaning to life is to grow. There is, therefore, no price too high to pay for growth. Not even your life. For growing is your life.

Growing is Life

appendices

APPENDIX A

FEELING WORD LIST*

Happy	Sad	Angry	Confused
alive	angry	aggravated	anxious
amused	apathetic	annoyed	awkward
anxious	awful	burned up	baffled
calm	bad	critical	bothered
cheerful	blue	disgusted	crazy
content	crushed	enraged	dazed
delighted	depressed	envious	depressed
ecstatic	disappointed	fed up	disorganized
excited	dissatisfied	frustrated	disoriented
fantastic	disturbed	furious	distracted
fine	down	impatient	disturbed
fortunate	embarrassed	irritated	embarrassed
friendly	gloomy	mad	frustrated
glad	glum	mean	helpless
good	hate	outraged	hopeless
great	hopeless	rage	lost
hopeful	hurt	resentful	mixed up
loving	lonely	sore	panicky
motherly	lost		paralyzed
optimistic	low		puzzled
peaceful	miserable		stuck
pleased	painful		surprised
proud	sorry		trapped
relaxed	terrible		troubled
relieved	turned off		uncertain
satisfied	uneasy		uncomfortable
thankful	unhappy		unsure
thrilled	unloved		upset
turned on	upset		weak
up			
warm			
wonderful			

*This list is in alphabetical order by feeling category. Since the intensity of any feeling word depends upon the person with whom it is used, you will need to visualize the typical helpee you work with to categorize these words by intensity level.

Scared	Weak	Strong
		active
afraid	ashamed	active
anxious	bored	aggressive
awed	confused	alert
chicken	defenseless	angry
confused	discouraged	bold
fearful	embarrassed	brave
frightened	exhausted	capable
horrified	fragile	confident
insecure	frail	determined
intimidated	frustrated	energetic
jumpy	guilty	happy
lonely	helpless	hate
nervous	horrible	healthy
panicky(ed)	ill	intense
shaky	impotent	loud
shy	inadequate	love
stunned	insecure	mean
tense	lifeless	open
terrified	lost	positive
threatened	overwhelmed	potent
timid	powerless	powerful
uneasy	quiet	quick
unsure	run-down	rage
worried	shaky	secure
	shy	solid
	sick	super
	timid	tough
	tired	
	unsure	
	useless	
	vulnerable	
	wish-washy	
	worn out	

APPENDIX B

A RESEARCH SUMMARY OF THE
EVOLUTION OF THE HELPING MODEL

Introduction

Perhaps the best way to enter a review of helping research is to appeal to your own experience. If you can take a moment, think about all of the teachers you have had. Of these 100 or so teachers, how many had a dramatic positive impact upon your life? How many facilitated your development in some significant way: where you found yourself able to do things that you were previously unable to do, or where you found totally new directions in your life? These were the facilitators or helpers you have known. If you are like the tens of thousands of people we have surveyed, you can identify three or four facilitative teachers out of the 100 in your experience. The range is from 0 to 10.

Conversely, how many of your teachers had a dramatic negative impact upon your life? How many retarded your development in some significant way: where you found yourself unable to do things you were previously able to do or where you were prevented from taking directions you knew you should take? These were the retarders or non-helpful people you have known. If you are like the people we have surveyed, you will recall four or five retarding teachers out of the 100 in your experience. The range is from 0 to 12.

How about those teachers who were neither facilitative nor retarding? You probably cannot recall their names or faces. You were like two ships passing in the night. Perhaps the greatest indictment of all is that 92 or 93 out of the 100 teachers you had did not make a difference. They did not do what they were paid to do: help you to grow and develop.

If you can recall these facilitative and retarding teachers, then you already know, in your personal experience, the effective ingredients of helping. Let us explore your experience further. What was it about the helping or learning process that distinguished the facilitative teachers from the retarding or neutral ones? If you say that the facilitative teachers really cared about you and tried to understand your experience, then you are like most people: you have identified one fundamental ingredient of helping — helper **responding** to facilitate helpee **understanding** of his or her experience. If you say that the facilitative teachers really had their content together so that they could help you to achieve your goals, then you have identified the other fundamental ingredient of helping — helper **initiating** to facilitate helpee **action** based upon the experience of the helpee.

You already know in your experience what it is to be accurately understood. You already know in your experience what it is to be helped to act effectively. You know, in your being, the effective ingredients of helping: **responding** accurately to another person's experience, and taking that other person's experience into consideration in **initiating** effectively from one's own experience. The following sections of this research summary will help to validate your experiences of effective helping. We will begin with the evolution of the research base which identified the dimensions of effective helping. Then we will describe the evolution of these dimensions into a more concrete form. Next we will discuss the specific helping skills which grew out of the core dimensions. Finally we will review the effects of teaching these skills to a variety of populations.

The Research Base

In the early 1960's, a number of challenges were issued to the helping professions (Eysenck, 1960, 1965; Levitt, 1963; Lewis, 1965). These challenges stated that counseling and psychotherapy did not make a difference. They discovered that both adults and children who were in control groups that were **not** assigned to professional practitioners, gained as much, **on the average,** as people assigned to professional counselors and therapists: about two-thirds of the patients improved and remained out of the hospital a year after treatment, **whether they were treated or not.**

This research was recently updated in longitudinal studies of more than 50 treatment settings by Anthony (1979). He studied the lasting effects of counseling, rehabilitation and psychotherapeutic techniques. He found that, within three to five years after treatment, 65 to 75 percent of the ex-patients were once again patients. Also, regardless of the follow-up period, the gainful employment of ex-patients was below twenty-five percent.

The major conclusion that might be drawn from these data is that counseling and psychotherapy — as traditionally practiced — are effective in about twenty percent of the cases. (Of the two-thrds of the clients and patients who eventually get better, only one-third to one quarter **stay** better. This means that psychotherapy has lasting positive effects in 17 to 22 percent of the cases.) To answer these challenges, further research was undertaken. We will examine the naturalistic studies of helping that led to predictive studies and, in turn, to the generalization and extension of an effective helping skills model.

Naturalistic Studies

One answer to the challenges to helping came from studying the natural variability of the professionally-treated groups. The clients and patients of professional helpers demonstrated a greater range of effects that those in professionally "untreated" groups (Rogers, et al, 1967; Truax and Carkhuff, 1967). This meant that professional practitioners tended to have a greater spread of effects on their patients: some got significantly better and some got worse. This finding suggested one very consoling conclusion: counseling and psychotherapy really did make a difference. It also suggested one very distressing conclusion: counseling and psychotherapy have a two-edged effect — they may be helpful or harmful (Bergin and Garfield, 1971).

Furthermore, the truly significant finding was that you could account, at least in part, for these helpful, neutral and harmful effects. The effects could be determined by the levels of functioning of the helpers on certain interpersonal dimensions such as empathy or empathic understanding. Counselors and therapists who offered high levels of a certain core of interpersonal dimensions facilitated the process movement of their clients and patients. And these same clients and patients got better. Those recipients of helpers offering low levels of understanding stayed the same or got worse (Rogers, et al, 1967; Truax and Carkhuff, 1967).

Predictive Studies

Following these early naturalistic studies, a number of predictive validity studies were conducted. These involved manipulating the levels of the helper's functioning on interpersonal dimensions such as empathy. The effects of these manipulations were studied both within the helping process and upon the helping outcomes. In general, within the helping process, the helpees (clients and patients) changed according to the helper's level of functioning: when the helpers offered high levels of interpersonal dimensions such as empathy, the helpees explored their problems in meaningful ways. When the helpers offered low levels of interpersonal dimensions, the helpees did not explore their problems in meaningful ways (Carkhuff and Alexik, 1967; Holder, et al, 1967; Piaget, et al, 1968; Truax and Carkhuff, 1967).

In the studies of helping outcomes, it was found that the helpees moved in the direction of the helpers' levels of functioning. In general, helpees of helpers functioning at high levels of these interpersonal dimensions moved toward higher levels of functioning. Helpees of helpers functioning at low levels of these interpersonal dimensions moved toward lower levels of functioning (Pagell, et al, 1967).

Generalization Studies

The next series of studies sought to generalize the effects of these interpersonal dimensions to other helping and human relationships. The first effort was to study the effects of teachers' levels of interpersonal functioning upon learners' development. Aspy and Roebuck (1972) divided teachers into high and low levels of interpersonal functioning and found significant relationships with student achievement indices such as Word Meaning, Paragraph Meaning, Spelling, Word Study Skills and Language. A number of subsequent studies were conducted assessing the relationship of interpersonal dimensions with a variety of other student outcome indices: the students of teachers offering high levels of these interpersonal dimensions demonstrated significant constructive gains in areas of emotional, interpersonal and intellectual functioning (Aspy and Roebuck, 1977).

These effects have been generalized in all areas of helping and human relationships where the "more knowing" person influences the "less knowing" person: parent-child relations (Carkhuff, 1971a; Carkhuff and Pierce, 1976); teacher-student relations (Aspy and Roebuck, 1977; Carkhuff, 1969); counselor-client relations (Berenson and Carkhuff, 1967; Carkhuff and Berenson, 1967); and therapist-patient relations (Anthony, 1979; Rogers, et al, 1967; Truax and Carkhuff, 1967). In general, the "less knowing" persons will move toward the levels of functioning of the "more knowing" persons over time, depending on both the extensiveness and intensity of contacts: helpees of high level functioning helpers get better on a variety of process and outcome indices, while helpees of low level functioning helpers get worse.

Extension Studies

Finally, a number of studies were conducted to extend the dimensions of helping. For example, Vitalo (1970) found that the effects of behavior modification programs were contingent, in part, upon the modifiers' levels of interpersonal functioning. Michelson and Stevic (1971) found that career information seeking behavior was dependent upon the helpers' levels of interpersonal functioning in interaction with their reinforcement programs. In general, those helpers who functioned at the highest levels, and had the most systematic helping programs, were most effective in helping their helpees.

Simultaneously, the core interpersonal dimensions were gradually extended and then factored into responsive and initiative dimensions (Berenson and Mitchell, 1974; Carkhuff, 1969). (Responsive dimensions respond to the helpee's experience. Initiative dimensions, while taking into consideration the helpee's experience, are generated from the helper's experience.) In addition, a number of systematic helping programs were developed to extend the helpers'

initiative activities to culminate in effective action programs
for the helpees (Carkhuff, 1969, 1971a).

In summary, those helping dimensions that appear
naturally in a limited number of effective helpers were
validated in predictive studies of both helping process and
outcome. In addition, the effectiveness of these helping
dimensions was generalized to all helping and human relationships. Finally, these dimensions were extended to equip
the helpers with more of the ingredients they needed to
effectively help others. The acceptance of these fundamental
ingredients of helping has been widely demonstrated in the
professional literature (Brammer, 1979; Combs, et al, 1978;
Danish and Hauer, 1973; Egan, 1975; Gazda, 1973; Gordon,
1975; Hackney and Cormier, 1979; Johnson, 1972; Okun,
1976; Patterson, 1973).

The Evolution of the Dimensions

Over a period of time, the core dimensions of helping
have evolved and been extended in a never-ending attempt to
account for helping effectiveness. What began with a gross
definition of the dimension of empathy, has evolved into an
extensive equation for human resource development. In
order to understand these dimensions, we must understand
four things: the **sources** of the helping dimensions as well as
their evolution, the helping **process** which these dimensions
impact, the helper **skills** which operationalize the dimensions,
and the helpee **outcomes** which these dimensions are in-
tended to achieve.

Helping Sources

There are two fundamental approaches to helping. One
may be called the insight approach. The other may be con-
ceived of as the action approach. The insight approach has
been supported by many traditional therapeutic schools.
In particular, the psychoanalytic, neoanalytic and client-
centered practitioners have emphasized the client's insight as
the basis for the development of an effective set of assumptions about his or her world (Adler, 1927; Freud, 1933;
Fromm, 1947; Horney, 1945; Jung, 1939; Rank, 1929;
Rogers, et al, 1967; Sullivan, 1938). The action approach

has been promulgated by the learning theory and behavior modification schools as well as the trait-and-factor school, which matches people to jobs and vice versa. These schools have emphasized the client's development and implementation of rational action plans for managing his or her world (Eysenck, 1960; Ginzberg et al, 1951; Krasner and Ullman, 1965; Parsons, 1909; Super, 1949; Watson, 1916; Wolpe, et al, 1964).

Unfortunately, both the insight and action approaches are incomplete without the other. Most insight approaches fail to develop the insights programmatically so that the client can "own" them. Even when they do, they fail to systematically develop action programs flowing from these insights. Similarly, while the action approaches develop their programs effectively, they fail to consolidate whatever behavior changes they have accomplished. They neglect to complement the action with insights so that the client can guide his or her own life (Carkhuff and Berenson, 1976, 1977). In order to effectively help human beings to change behavior, the insight and action approaches must be integrated into one effective helping process.

Helping Process

In order to demonstrate a change or gain in behavior, the helpees must **act** differently from the way they did before. In order to act effectively, the helpees must have insights or **understand** accurately their goals and the ways to achieve them. In order to understand their goals, the helpees must **explore** their world experientially. These three learning or re-learning processes are the phases of helping through which the helpees must be guided (Carkhuff and Berenson, 1976).

The helpees must first **explore** where they are in relation to their worlds and the significant people in their worlds. They must next **understand** where they are in relation to where they want to be. Finally, they must **act** to get from where they are to where they want to be. With the feedback from their action, they can recycle the learning process for more extensive exploration, more accurate understanding and more effective action (Carkhuff and Berenson, 1976).

Helper Skills

In order to be effective in helping, then, the helper skills must facilitate the helpee's movement through the three-phase helping process. The historic dimension of empathy was complemented by unconditional positive regard and genuineness (Rogers, et al, 1967). These dimensions were transformed by more operational definitions into accurate empathy, respect and genuineness (Carkhuff, 1969; Truax and Carkhuff, 1967). They were, in turn, complemented by other dimensions including specificity or concreteness, self-disclosure, confrontation, and immediacy and, then, factored into responsive and initiative dimensions (Berenson and Mitchell, 1974; Carkhuff, 1969).

The responsive dimensions (empathy, respect, specifity of expression) responded to the helpee's experience and, thus, facilitated the helpee's movement toward understanding. The initiative dimensions (genuineness, self-disclosure, confrontation, immediacy, and concreteness) were generated from the helper's experience and stimulated the helpee's movement toward action (Berenson and Mitchell, 1974; Carkhuff, 1971a). These initiative dimensions were later extended to incorporate the problem-solving skills and program development skills needed to fully help the helpees to achieve appropriate outcomes (Carkhuff 1974b, 1975; Carkhuff and Anthony, 1979).

Helpee Outcomes

In the early research, the helpee outcomes emphasized the emotional changes or gains of the helpees. Since the helping methods were insight-oriented, the process emphasized helpee exploration, and the outcome assessments measured the changes in the helpee's level of emotional insights (Rogers, et al, 1967; Truax and Carkhuff, 1967). Clearly, these emotional outcomes were restrictive because they were assessing only one dimension of the helpee's functioning.

These outcomes were later defined more broadly to incorporate all dimensions of human resource development to which the helping process is dedicated. The emotional dimension was extended to incorporate the interpersonal functioning of the helpees (Carkhuff, 1969, 1971a). The dimension of physical functioning was added to measure relevant data on the helpees' fitness and energy levels (Collingwood, 1972). The intellectual dimension was added to measure the helpees' intellectual achievement and capabilities (Aspy and Roebuck, 1972, 1977).

In summary, helping effectiveness is a function of the helper's skills to facilitate the helping process to accomplish helping outcomes. Helping outcomes include the physical, emotional and intellectual dimensions of human resource development. The helping process, by which outcomes are accomplished, emphasizes the helpee's exploration, understanding and acting. The helping skills, by which the process is facilitated, include responding and initiating skills.

The Helping Skills

The responsive and initiative factors of helping dominate the helping process. They facilitate the exploration, understanding and action that culminate in the physical, emotional and intellectual helpee outcomes. As a result of attempts to teach helpers how to accomplish these processes and outcomes, the responsive and initiative dimensions were further refined into concrete helping skills. These helping skills are called attending, responding, personalizing and initiating. The attending skills are preparatory to responding, and the personalizing skills are transitional between responding and initiating.

Attending Skills

Attending skills involve communicating a "hovering attentiveness" to the helpee. By attending physically, the helper communicates interest in the helpee's welfare. By observing and listening, the helper learns from and about the helpee. Attending is the richest source of learning about the helpee (Barker, 1971; Birdwhistell, 1967; Ekman, et al, 1972; Garfield, 1971; Genther and Moughan, 1977, Genther and Sacuzzo, 1977; Hall, 1959, 1976; Ivey, 1971, 1978; Mehrabian, 1972; Schefflen, 1969; Smith-Hanen, 1977).

Within the helping process, attending serves to facilitate the helpee's involvement in helping. By communicating interest in the helpee, the helper establishes the conditions for the helpee's involvement in the helping process. Reduced to their minimum, attending skills may be seen as the acts of being decent to the helpee in a world that is very often indecent (Carkhuff and Berenson, 1976).

Responding Skills

Basic responding skills involve the helper's accurate understanding of the helpee's experience. They include first discriminating and then communicating the content and feelings of the helpee's experience. When employed at levels interchangeable with the helpee's experience, they serve to insure that the helper is fully in tune with the helpee (Aspy and Roebuck, 1977; Carkhuff, 1969; Carkhuff and Berenson, 1967, 1977; Rogers, et al, 1967; Truax and Carkhuff, 1967).

Responding skills serve to stimulate the helpee's exploration of where he or she is in his or her experience of the world. The accurate response becomes a mirror image of the helpee's experience. Responding skills also serve to reinforce the helpee's exploration by showing the helpee that the helper is fully in tune with the helpee's experience (Carkhuff and Berenson, 1976).

Personalizing Skills

Personalizing skills involve responding to the personal implications of the meaning, problem, feeling and, finally, the goal. The helper processes the learnings from helpee exploration and initiates movement toward understanding through a consideration of personalized implications. Personalizing skills culminate in the helpee's personal experience of the problem as the inability to handle difficult situations (Adler, 1927; Anthony, 1971; Berenson and Mitchell, 1974; Binswanger, 1956; Carkhuff, 1969; Carkhuff and Berenson, 1976; Freud, 1933; Fromm, 1947; Heidegger, 1962; Horney, 1945; Jung, 1939; May, 1961; Rank, 1929; Sullivan, 1948).

Personalizing skills are used to provide a transition from responding to initiating and from exploring to acting. When

employed effectively, they facilitate the helpee's understanding of where he or she wants to be in the world. They
serve to focus upon the helpee's goals which are the basis for
acting (Carkhuff and Berenson, 1976).

Initiating Skills

Finally, initiating skills involve operationalizing the goals,
and then developing and implementing the steps to achieve
these goals. Again, remember that the goals are calculated to
resolve the helpee's problems. Most simply, initiative skills
foster the development and implementation of the mechanical steps that are required to achieve the personally meaningful goals that the helpee has developed (Authier, et al, 1975;
Carkhuff, 1969, 1971b; 1974b; 1975; Carkhuff and Anthony,
1979; Collingwood, et al, 1978; Goldstein, 1976; Ivey, 1976;
Sprinthall and Mosher, 1971).

The initiating skills conclude the first cycle of the helping
process. The helper employs initiative skills to stimulate the
helpee's acting to achieve his or her goals. When employed
effectively, initiative skills facilitate the helpee's acting to
get to where he or she wants to be in the world (Carkhuff
and Berenson, 1976).

In summary: the attending skills serve to involve the
helpee in helping; responding skills facilitate exploration;
personalizing skills facilitate understanding; and initiating
skills stimulate acting. Again, with the feedback from acting,
the helping or learning process is recycled until the goals are
achieved and the problems are resolved.

The Training Applications

It was a natural step to train helpers in helping skills and
study the effects on helping outcomes. Indeed, the development of both the skills technologies and the training systems
was a highly interactional process, with each refining the
other and both, in turn, being shaped by their outcomes.
It was also only natural that the first of these training applications take place with credentialed counselors and therapists.
Next came the training of lay and indigenous helper populations, followed by the direct training of helpee populations
to service themselves.

Credentialed Helpers

The first series of training applications demonstrated that professional helpers could be trained to function at levels commensurate with "outstanding" practitioners (Truax & Carkhuff, 1967). In a later series, it was established that credentialed professionals could, in the brief time of 100 hours or less, learn to function above minimally effective and self-sustaining levels of interpersonal skills, levels beyond those offered by most "outstanding" practitioners (Carkhuff, 1969). Perhaps most importantly, trained counselors were able to involve their counselees in the helping process at levels that led to constructive change or gain. In one demonstration study in guidance, against a very low base success rate of 13 to 25 percent, the trained counselors were able to demonstrate success rates between 74 and 91 percent (Carkhuff and Berenson, 1976, Chapter 9).

A series of training applications in teaching soon followed. Hefele (1971) found student achievement to be a function of systematic training of teachers in helping skills. Berenson (1971) found that experimentally-trained teachers were rated significantly higher in interpersonal skills and competency in the classroom than were other teachers who received a variety of control conditions (including a training control group, a Hawthorne Effect control group and a control group proper). Aspy and Roebuck (1977), building upon their earlier work, have continued to employ a variety of teacher training strategies demonstrating the positive effects of helping skills upon student physical, emotional and intellectual functioning.

Functional Professionals

It is clear that a dimension such as interpersonal functioning is not the exclusive province of credentialed professionals. Lay personnel can learn as well as professionals to be caring and empathic in their relations with helpee populations. With this growing recognition, a number of training applications using lay personnel were conducted. The majority of these programs dealt with staff personnel.

Staff personnel, such as nurses and hospital attendants, policemen and prison guards, dormitory counselors and community volunteers, were trained and their effects in treatment studied. The effects were very positive for both the staff and helpee populations for, after all, the line staff and helpee populations were those who lived most intimately with each other. In general, the lay helpers were able to elicit significant changes in work behaviors, discharge rates, recidivism rates and a variety of other areas including self-reports, significant-other-reports and expert-reports (Carkhuff, 1969, 1971a; Carkhuff & Berenson, 1976).

Indigenous Personnel

The difference between functional professional staff and indigenous functional professionals is the difference between the attendant and the patient, the policeman and the delinquent, the guard and the inmate and the teacher and the student. That is to say, indigenous personnel are part of the community being serviced. It is a natural extension of the lay helper training principle to train helpee recipients as well as staff.

Here the research indicates that, with systematic selection and training, indigenous functional professionals can work effectively with the populations from which they are drawn. For example, human relations specialists drawn from recipient ranks have facilitated school and work adjustments for troubled populations. New careers teachers, themselves drawn from the ranks of the unemployed, have systematically helped others to learn the skills they needed in order to get and hold meaningful jobs (Carkhuff, 1971a).

Helpee Populations

The logical culmination of helper training is to train helpee populations directly in the kinds of skills which they need to service themselves. Thus, parents of emotionally disturbed children were systematically trained in the skills which they needed to function effectively with themselves and their children (Carkhuff and Bierman, 1970). Patients were trained to offer each other rewarding human rela-

tionships. The results were significantly more positive
than all other forms of treatment, including individual or
group therapy, drug treatment or "total push" treatment
(Pierce and Drasgow, 1969). Training was, indeed, the
preferred mode of treatment!

The concept of training as treatment led directly to
the development of programs to train entire communities to
create a therapeutic milieu. This has been accomplished most
effectively in institutional-type settings where staff and resi-
dents are trained in the kinds of skills necessary to work
effectively with each other. Thus, both institutional and
community-based criminal justice settings have yielded data
indicating reduced recidivism and increased employability
(Carkhuff, 1974a; Collingwood, et al, 1978; Montgomery and
Brown, 1980).

In summary, both lay staff and indigenous personnel may
be selected and trained as functional professional helpers.
In these roles, they can effect any human resource development that professionals can — and more! Further, directly
teaching the helpee populations the kinds of skills which they
need to service themselves is a direct extension of the helper
principle. When we train people in the skills which they need
to function effectively in their worlds, we increase the probability that they will, in fact, begin to live, learn and work in
increasingly constructive ways.

Summary and Conclusions

We began the research summary with your personal experiences of facilitative and retarding teachers—experiences
which we all have in common. We discovered that you know,
experientially, the ingredients of helpfulness: caring, empathic people (responsiveness) who can help you accomplish
your goals and resolve your problems (initiative). We have
devoted the remainder of the discussion to validating your
experience. We have discussed the evolution of the helping
research, the extension and operationalization of the helping
dimensions, and a variety of training applications. We have
learned many facts, concepts and principles about helping.

We have found that all helping and human relationships may be "for better or for worse." The effects depend upon the helper's level of skills in facilitating the helpee's movement through the helping process toward constructive helping outcomes. These responsive and initiative helping skills constitute the core of all helping experiences.

The helping skills may be used in all one-to-one and one-to-group relationships. They are used in conjunction with the helper's specialty skills in counseling, teaching and working. They may be used in conjunction with any of a number of potential preferred modes of treatment, drawn from a variety of helping orientations, to meet the helpee's needs. Finally, the same skills may be taught directly to the helpees in order to help them help themselves: teaching clients skills is the preferred mode of treatment for most helpee populations.

In conclusion, the helping skills will enable you to have helpful rather than harmful effects upon the people with whom you relate. We can learn to become effective helpers with success rates ranging upwards from two-thirds to over ninety percent, against a base success rate of around twenty percent. Most importantly, we can use these skills to help ourselves and others to become healthy human beings and to form healthy human relationships.

The only assumption that we have made in developing the helping skills programs involves your motivation. Our assumption is that you want to grow, that you want to be like the facilitative helpers and teachers you have experienced, that you want to become involved in a life-long learning process.

You have explored many facts, concepts and principles about helping. You know where you are. You also understand the skills which you need to learn to become an effective helper — indeed, an effective human. You know where you want to be. It remains for you to commit yourself to acquiring and applying the skill steps that will make you an effective helper. You know how to act to get there.

REFERENCES

Adler, A. *Understanding human nature.* New York: Wolfe & Greenberg Publishers, 1927.

Anthony, W. A. A methodological investigation of the "minimally facilitative level of interpersonal function." *Journal of Clinical Psychology,* 1971, *27,* 156-157.

Anthony, W. A. *The Principles of Psychiatric Rehabilitation.* Baltimore, MD: University Park Press, 1979.

Aspy, D. N. and Roebuck, F. N. An investigation of the relationship between levels of cognitive functioning and the teacher's classroom behavior. *Journal of Educational Research,* May, 1972.

Aspy, D. N. and Roebuck, F. N. *KIDS don't learn from people they don't like.* Amherst, Mass.: Human Resource Development Press, 1977.

Authier, J., Gustafson, K., Guerney, B. and Kasdorf, J. A. The psychological practitioner as a teacher. *Counseling Psychologist,* 1975, *5,* 31-50.

Barker, L. L. *Listening behavior.* Englewood Cliffs, N.J.: Prentice-Hall, 1971.

Berenson, B. G. and Carkhuff, R. R. *Sources of gain in counseling and psychotherapy.* New York: Holt, Rinehart & Winston, 1967.

Berenson, B. G. and Mitchell, K. M. *Confrontation: for better or worse.* Amherst, Mass.: Human Resource Development Press, 1974.

Berenson, D. H. The effects of systematic human relations training upon the classroom performance of elementary school teachers. *Journal of Research and Development in Education,* 1971, *4,* 70-85.

Bergin, A. E. and Garfield, S. L. (Eds.) *Handbook of psychotherapy and behavioral change.* New York: John Wiley & Sons, 1971.

Binswanger, L. Existential analysis and psychotherapy. In F. Fromm-Reichman and J. L. Moreno (Eds.). *Progress in psychotherapy.* New York: Grune & Stratton, 1956.

Birdwhistell, R. Some body motion elements accompanying spoken American English. In L. Thayer (Ed.), *Communication: Concepts and Perspectives.* Washington, D.C.: Spartan, 1967.

Brammer, L. *The helping relationship,* 2nd ed., Englewood Cliffs, N.J.: Prentice-Hall, 1979.

Carkhuff, R. R. *Helping and human relations,* Volumes I & II. New York: Holt, Rinehart & Winston, 1969.

Carkhuff, R. R. *The development of human resources.* New York: Holt, Rinehart & Winston, 1971 (a).

Carkhuff, R. R. Training as a preferred mode of treatment. *Journal of Counseling Psychology,* 1971 (b), *18,* 123-131.

Carkhuff, R. R. *Cry twice.* Amherst, Mass.: Human Resource Development Press, 1974 (a).

Carkhuff, R. R. *The art of problem-solving.* Amherst, Mass.: Human Resource Development Press, 1974 (b).

Carkhuff, R. R. *The art of program development.* Amherst, Mass.: Human Resource Development Press, 1975.

Carkhuff, R. R. and Alexik, M. The effects of the manipulation of client depth of self-exploration upon high and low functioning counselors. *Journal of Clinical Psychology,* 1967, *23,* 210-212.

Carkhuff, R. R. and Anthony W. A. *The skills of helping.* Amherst, Mass.: Human Resource Development Press, 1979.

Carkhuff, R. R. and Becker, J. *Toward excellence in education.* Amherst, Mass.: Carkhuff Institute of Human Technology, 1977.

Carkhuff, R. R. and Berenson, B. G. *Beyond counseling and therapy,* New York: Holt, Rinehart & Winston, 1967, 1977.

Carkhuff, R. R. and Berenson, B. G. *Teaching as treatment.* Amherst, Mass.: Human Resource Development Press, 1976.

Carkhuff, R. R. and Bierman, R. Training as a preferred mode of treatment of parents of emotionally disturbed children. *Journal of Counseling Psychology.* 1970, *17,* 157-161.

Carkhuff, R. R. and Pierce R. M. *Helping begins at home.* Amherst, Mass.: Human Resource Development Press, 1976.

Collingwood, T. HRD model and physical fitness. *In HRD Model in Education,* D. W. Kratochvil, (Ed.), Baton Rouge, La.: Southern University, 1972.

Collingwood, T., Douds, A., Williams, H., and Wilson, R. *Developing youth resources.* Amherst, Mass.: Carkhuff Institute of Human Technology, 1978.

Combs, A., Avila D. and Purkey, W. *Helping relationships: Basic concepts for the helping professions.* Boston: Allyn and Bacon, 1978.

Danish, S. and Hauer, A. *Helping skills: A basic training program.* New York: Behavioral Publications, 1973.

Egan, G. *The skilled helper.* Monterey Calif.: Brooks Cole, 1975.

Ekman, P., Friesen, W., and Ellworth, P. *Emotion in the human face.* New York: Pergammon, 1972.

Eysenck, H. J. The effects of psychotherapy, In H. J. Eysenck (Ed.), *The handbook of abnormal psychology,* New York: Basic Books, 1960.

Eysenck, H. J. The effects of psychotherapy. *Int. J. Psychother.,* 1965, *1,* 99-178.

Freud, S. *New introductory lectures.* New York: Norton, 1933.

Fromm, E. *Man for himself.* New York: Holt, Rinehart & Winston, 1947.

Garfield, S. Research on client variables in psychotherapy. In A. E. Bergin and S. L. Garfield (Eds.), *Handbook of psychotherapy and behavioral change.* New York: Wiley & Sons, 1971.

Gazda, G. *Human relations development.* Boston: Allyn and Bacon, 1973.

Genther, R. & Moughan, J. Introverts' and extraverts' responses to non-verbal attending behavior. *Journal of Counseling Psychology,* 1977, *24,* 144-146.

Genther, R. and Saccuzzo, D. Accuracy of perceptions of psychotherapeutic content as a function of observers' levels of facilitation. *Journal of Clinical Psychology,* 1977, *33,* 517-519.

Ginzberg, E., Ginsburg, S. W., Axelrad, S., and Herma, J. L. *Occupational choice.* New York: Columbia University Press, 1951.

Goldstein, A., Sprafkin, R., and Gershaw, N. *Skill training for community living.* New York: Pergammon Press, 1976.

Gordon, R. *Interviewing: Strategy, techniques and tactics.* Homewood, Ill.: Dorsey Press, 1975.

Hackney, H. and Cormier, L. *Counseling strategies and objectives,* 2nd ed. Englewood Cliffs, N.J.: Prentice Hall, 1979.

Hall, E. *The silent language.* New York: Doubleday, 1959.

Hall, E. *Beyond culture.* New York: Doubleday, 1976.

Hefele, T. J. The effects of systematic human relations training upon student achievement. *Journal of Research and Development in Education,* 1971, *4,* 52-69.

Heidegger, M. *Being and time.* London: SCM Press, 1962.

Holder, T., Carkhuff, R. R. and Berenson, B. G. The differential effects of the manipulation of therapeutic conditions upon high and low functioning clients. *Journal of Counseling Psychology,* 1967, *14,* 63-66.

Horney, K. *Our inner conflicts.* New York: Norton, 1945.

Ivey, A. The counselor as teacher. *Personnel and Guidance Journal,* 1976, *54,* 431-434.

Ivey, A. and Authier, J. *Microcounseling.* Springfield, III.: Thomas, 1971, 1978.

Johnson, D. *Reaching out: Interpersonal effectiveness and self-actualization.* Englewood Cliffs, N.J.: Prentice Hall, 1972.

Jung, C. *The integration of the personality.* New York: Holt, Rinehart & Winston, 1939.

Krasner, L., and L. Ullmann. *Research in Behavior Modification.* New York: Holt, Rinehart and Winston, 1965.

Levitt, E. E. Psychotherapy with children: A further evaluation. *Behavior Research and Therapy,* 1963, *1,* 45-51.

Lewis, W. W. Continuity and intervention in emotional disturbance: A review. *Exceptional Children,* 1965, *31,* 465-475.

May, R. (Ed.). *Existential psychology.* New York: Random House, 1961.

Mehrabian, A. *Nonverbal communication.* New York: Aldine-Atherton, 1972.

Mickelson, D. J. and Stevic, R. R. Differential effects of facilitative and non-facilitative behavioral counselors. *Journal of Counseling Psychology,* 1971, *18,* 314-319.

Montgomery, C. and Brown, A. *In the land of the blind.* Amherst, Mass.: Carkhuff Institute of Human Technology, in press, 1980.

Okun, B. *Effective helping: Interviewing and counseling techniques.* North Scituate, Mass.: Duxbury Press, 1976.

Pagell, W., Carkhuff, R. R. and Berenson, B. G. The predicted differential effects of the level of counselor functioning upon the level of functioning of outpatients. *Journal of Clinical Psychology,* 1967, *23,* 510-512.

Parsons, F. *Choosing a vocation.* Boston: Houghton Mifflin, 1909.

Patterson, C. *Theories of counseling and psychotherapy,* 2nd ed. New York: Harper and Row, 1973.

Piaget, G., Carkhuff, R. R. and Berenson, B. G. The development of skills in interpersonal functioning. *Counselor Education and Supervision,* 1968, *2,* 102-106.

Pierce, R. M. and Drasgow, J. Teaching facilitative interpersonal functioning to psychiatric inpatients. *Journal of Counseling Psychology,* 1969, *16,* 295-298.

Rank, O. *The trauma of birth.* New York: Harcourt, 1929.

Rogers, C., Gendlin, E., Keisler, D., and Truax, C. *The therapeutic relationship and its impact.* Westport, Conn.: Greenwood Press, 1967.

Schefflen, A. *Stream and structure of communication behavior.* Bloomington, Ind.: Purdue University Press, 1969.

Smith-Hanen, S. Nonverbal behavior and counselor warmth and empathy. *Journal of Counseling Psychology,* 1977, *24,* 87-91.

Sprinthall, N. and Mosher, R. Psychological education: A means to promote personal development during adolescence. *The Counseling Psychologist,* 1971, *2*(4), 3-84.

Sullivan, H. The meaning of anxiety in psychiatry and life. *Psychiatry,* 1948, *11*(1).

Super, D. E. *Appraising vocational fitness.* New York: Harper & Row, 1949.

Truax, C. B. and Carkhuff, R. R. *Toward effective counseling and psychotherapy.* Chicago: Aldine, 1967.

Vitalo, R. The effects of facilitative interpersonal functioning in a conditioning paradigm. *Journal of Counseling Psychology,* 1970, *17,* 141-144.

Watson, J. B. Behaviorism and the concept of mental disease. *J. Phil. Psychol.,* 1916, *13,* 589-597.

Wolpe, J., A. Salter, and L. Renya. *The conditioning therapies.* New York: Holt, Rinehart and Winston, 1964.

APPENDIX C

ANNOTATED BIBLIOGRAPHY

Research

Anthony, W. A.
The Principles of Psychiatric Rehabilitation
Baltimore, MD: University Park Press, 1979
Useful for professionals engaged in the practice of psychiatric rehabilitation in community mental health centers and clinics. Concludes that the key to successful psychiatric rehabilitation is the skill level of the practitioner not where the helpee is treated. An outline of the skills necessary along with a summary of the research supporting each skill is also included.

Aspy, D. N. and Roebuck, F. N.
Kids Don't Learn from People They Don't Like
Amherst, Mass.: Human Resource Development Press, 1977
Useful for understanding the research base for the Carkhuff Model in teaching. Hundreds of teachers were trained in interpersonal skills. The effects on thousands of learners were studied. Significant gains were achieved on the following indices: student absenteeism and tardiness; student discipline and school crises; student learning skills and cognitive growth. Concludes that the Carkhuff Model is the preferred teacher training model.

Berenson, B. G.
Belly-to-Belly and Back-to-Back: The Militant Humanism of Robert R. Carkhuff
Amherst, Mass.: Human Resource Development Press, 1975
Useful for an understanding of the human assumptions underlying the human resource development models of Carkhuff. Presents a collection of prose and poetry by Carkhuff. Concludes by challenging us to die growing.

Berenson, B. G. and Carkhuff, R. R.
The Sources of Gain in Counseling and Psychotherapy
New York: Holt, Rinehart & Winston, 1967
Useful for an in-depth view of the different orientations to helping. Integrates the research of diverse approaches to helping. Concludes with a model of core conditions around which the different preferred modes of treatment make their own unique contributions to helpee benefits.

Berenson, B. G. and Mitchell, K. M.
Confrontation: For Better or Worse
Amherst, Mass.: Human Resource Development Press, 1974
Useful for an in-depth view of confrontation and immediacy
as well as the core interpersonal dimensions. Presents extensive
experimental manipulation of core interpersonal skills and
confrontation and immediacy. Concludes that while confrontation is never necessary and never sufficient, in the hands of
an effective helper, it may be efficient for moving the helpee
toward constructive gain or change.

Carkhuff, R. R.
**Helping and Human Relations. 1. Selection and Training. 2. Prac-
tice and Research**
New York: Holt, Rinehart & Winston, 1969
Useful for understanding the research base for interpersonal
skills in counseling and education. Operationalizes the helping
process in great detail. Presents extensive research evidence
for systematic selection, training and treatment procedures.
Concludes that teaching is the preferred mode of treatment
for helping.

Carkhuff, R. R.
The Development of Human Resources
New York: Holt, Rinehart & Winston, 1971
Useful for understanding applications of human resource
development (HRD) models. Describes and presents research
evidence for numerous applications of helping skills training
in human, educational and community resource development.
Concludes that systematic planning for human delivery
systems can be effectively translated into human benefits.

Carkhuff, R.R. and Becker, J.W.
Toward Excellence in Education
Amherst, Mass.: Carkhuff Institute of Human Technology, 1977
Useful for understanding the ingredients of effective education,
including: teachers; learners; parents; administrators; and the
community. Concludes that a human technology is required to
bridge the gap from our concepts of teaching to our deliveries
of learning.

Carkhuff, R.R. and Becker, J.W.
The Day·the Schools Closed Down
Amherst, Mass.: Carkhuff Institute of Human Technology, 1978
Useful for understanding the interaction of different systems
affecting human resource development: resource systems;
government systems; economic systems; educational systems.
Concludes that a human achievement system based upon a
human technology can affect the other systems constructively.

Carkhuff, R. R., Devine, J., Berenson, B. G., Griffin, A. H., Angelone, R., Keeling, T., Patch, W. and Steinberg, H.
   Cry Twice!
   Amherst, Mass.: Human Resource Development Press, 1974
      Useful for understanding the ingredients of institutional change. Details the people, programs and organizational variables needed to transform an institution from a custodial to a treatment orientation. Concludes that institutional change begins with people change.

Collingwood, T., Douds, A., Williams, H., and Wilson, R.D.
   Developing Youth Resources Through Police Diversion
   Amherst, Mass.: Carkhuff Institute of Human Technology, 1978
      Useful for understanding the effective ingredients of delinquency prevention and youth rehabilitation. The purpose of the program described was to provide services at the police level to juvenile offenders in order to reduce recidivism by delivering skills training and by monitoring services to youth and parents. Concludes that with systematic skills training programs, with skilled personnel, and with an organizational framework in a police department, you can make a dramatic and constructive impact on juvenile offender recidivism.

Carkhuff, R. R. and Berenson, B. G.
   Beyond Counseling and Therapy
   New York: Holt, Rinehart & Winston, Second Edition, 1977
      Useful for understanding of the core interpersonal conditions and their implications and applications. Adds many core dimensions and factors them out as responsive and initiative dimensions. Includes an analysis of the client-centered, existential, psychoanalytic, trait-and-factor and behavioristic orientations to counseling and psychotherapy. Concludes that only the trait-and-factor and behavioristic positions make unique contributions to human benefits over and above the core conditions.

Carkhuff, R. R. and Berenson, B. G.
   Teaching as Treatment
   Amherst, Mass.: Human Resource Development Press, 1976
      Useful for understanding the development of a human technology. Operationalizes the helping process as teaching. Offers research evidence for living, learning and working skills development and physical, emotional and intellectual outcomes. Concludes that learning-to-learn is the fundamental model for living, learning and working.

Rogers, C. R., Gendlin, E. T., Kiesler, D. and Truax, C. B.
   The Therapeutic Relationship and Its Impact
   Madison, Wis.: University of Wisconsin Press, 1967
      Useful for understanding the historical roots of the HRD

models. Presents extensive evidence on client-centered counseling for schizophrenic patients. Concludes that core interpersonal dimensions of empathy, regard and congruence are
critical to effective helping.

Truax, C. B. and Carkhuff, R. R.
Toward Effective Counseling and Therapy
Chicago: Aldine, 1967
Useful for understanding the transitional phases in developing HRD models. Presents extensive evidence on training lay
and professional helpers as well as different orientations to
helping. Concludes that the core interpersonal dimensions of
empathy, respect and genuineness are critical to effective
helping.

Skills Development and Applications

Living Skills

Carkhuff, R. R., Pierce, R. M., Banks, G. P., Berenson, D. H.,
Cannon, J. R., Zigon, F. J.
The Art of Helping IV — Trainer's Guide
Amherst, Mass.: Human Resource Development Press,
1980
Useful training techniques for teaching helpers. Includes attending, responding, personalizing and
initiating learning exercises with counseling applications.

Carkhuff, R. R., Cannon, J. R., Decker, D., Pierce, R. M.,
Schoenecker, C. M., Zigon, F. J.
The Art of Helping IV — Student Workbook
Amherst, Mass.: Human Resource Development Press,
1980
Useful for bridging the gap between reading about
helping skills in the text and practicing the skills in
training sessions. Includes hundreds of practice exer-
cises for Attending, Responding, Personalizing and
Initiating skills.

Carkhuff, R. R., Anthony, W. A., Cannon, J. R., Pierce,
R. M., Zigon, F. J.
The Skills of Helping
Amherst, Mass.: Human Resource Development Press,
1979
Useful for training helpers in helping skills. Includes
Attending, Responding, Personalizing, Problem Solv-
ing, Program Development and Initiating Skills.

Carkhuff, R. R., Anthony, W. A., Cannon, J. R., Pierce,
R. M., Schoenecker, C. M., Decker, D., Zigon, F. J.
   The Skills of Helping — Student Workbook
   Amherst, Mass.: Human Resource Development Press,
   1980
      Useful companion to Skills of Helping textbook de-
      signed to bridge the gap between reading about the
      skills and practicing them in class. Includes hundreds
      of practice exercises for interpersonal, Problem
      Solving and Program Development skills.

Carkhuff, R. R.
   The Art of Problem-Solving
   Amherst, Mass.: Human Resource Development Press,
   1973
      Useful for developing decision-making skills. In-
      cludes modules on defining problems and goals and
      selecting and implementing courses of action.

Carkhuff, R. R.
   The Art of Program Development
   Amherst, Mass.: Human Resource Development Press,
   1974
      Useful for developing program development skills.
      Includes modules on defining goals and developing
      and implementing programs to achieve the goals.

Teaching Skills

Carkhuff, R. R., Berenson, D. H. and Pierce, R. M.
   The Skills of Teaching: Interpersonal Skills
   Amherst, Mass.: Human Resource Development Press,
   1977
      Useful for pre-service and inservice teachers. Includes
      attending, responding, personalizing and initiating
      modules with classroom applications.

Berenson, D. H., Carkhuff, R. R. and Pierce, R. M.
   The Skills of Teaching — Teacher's Guide
   Amherst, Mass.: Human Resource Development Press,
   1977
      Useful training skills for teacher trainers. Includes
      methods for developing content and delivering inter-
      personal skills modules.

Berenson, D.H., Berenson, S.R., and Carkhuff, R.R.
   The Skills of Teaching: Content Development Skills
   Amherst, Mass.: Human Resource Development Press, 1978
      Useful for both preservice and inservice teacher education.
      Includes how to develop and organize both yearly and daily
      teaching content and how to identify skills and the steps needed
      to do them, along with the facts, concepts and principles stu-
      dents will need to perform these skills.

Berenson, D.H., Berenson, S.R., and Carkhuff, R.R.
The Skills of Teaching: Lesson Planning Skills
Amherst, Mass.: Human Resource Development Press, 1978
Useful for teaching both preservice and inservice teachers.
Includes how to select a piece of content and develop a lesson
plan to deliver it using teaching methods to review, overview,
present, practice and summarize.

Berenson, S.R., Berenson, D.H., and Carkhuff, R.R.
The Skills of Teaching: Teaching Delivery Skills
Amherst, Mass.: Human Resource Development Press, 1979
Useful for both inservice and preservice teacher education programs. Includes a summary and integrative presentation of
content development skills, lesson planning skills and interpersonal skills as applied to actual teaching delivery.

Working Skills

Carkhuff, R. R. and Friel, T. W.
The Art of Developing a Career—Student's Guide
Amherst, Mass.: Human Resource Development Press, 1974
Useful for developing careers. Includes modules on expanding,
narrowing and planning for career alternatives.

Carkhuff, R. R., Pierce, R. M., Friel, T. W. and Willis, D.
GETAJOB
Amherst, Mass.: Human Resource Development Press, 1975
Useful for developing placement skills. Includes modules on
finding jobs, preparing resumes and handling job interviews.

Friel, T. W. and Carkhuff, R. R.
The Art of Developing a Career—Helper's Guide
Amherst, Mass.: Human Resource Development Press, 1974
Useful training skills for helpers and teachers. Includes
methods for involving the learners in exploring, understand-
ing and acting upon their careers.

Fitness Skills

Collingwood, T. and Carkhuff, R. R.
Get Fit for Living
Amherst, Mass.: Human Resource Development Press, 1976
Useful for developing physical fitness. Includes modules for
self-assessing, setting goals and developing and implementing
fitness programs.

Collingwood, T. and Carkhuff, R. R.
Get Fit for Living—Trainer's Guide
Amherst, Mass.: Human Resource Development Press, 1976
Useful training skills for fitness trainers. Includes methods
and programs for delivering fitness skills.

Applications

Anthony, W. A. and Carkhuff, R. R.
The Art of Health Care
Amherst, Mass.: Human Resource Development Press, 1976
Useful for health care workers. Includes modules and applications of interpersonal, decision-making and program development skills in health care facilities.

Anthony, W.A., Cohen, M.R., Pierce, R.M., Cannon, J.R., Cohen, B.F., Friel, T.W., Spaniol, L., and Vitalo, R.L.
The Psychiatric Rehabilitation Practice Series (6 vols + instructor's guide) Baltimore, MD: University Park Press, 1979
Useful for inservice and preservice training of psychiatric rehabilitation practitioners. Includes volumes on diagnostic planning, rehabilitation programming, professional evaluation, career counseling, career placement and community service coordination.

Carkhuff, R. R. and Pierce, R. M.
Teacher as Person
Washington, D.C.: National Education Association, 1976
Useful for teachers interested in multi-cultural education. Includes modules and applications of interpersonal skills in the school.

Carkhuff, R. R. and Pierce, R. M.
Helping Begins at Home
Amherst, Mass.: Human Resource Development Press, 1976
Useful for parents interested in parenting skills. Includes modules and applications of interpersonal and program development skills in the home.

The books in the preceding Annotated Bibliography can be purchased directly from the publishers:

Aldine Publishing Company
529 South Wabash Ave.
Chicago, IL 60605

Carkhuff Institute of Human Technology
22 Amherst Road
Amherst, MA 01002

Greenwood Press
51 Riverside Ave.
Westport, CT 06880

Holt, Rinehart and Winston
383 Madison Ave.
New York, New York 10019

Human Resource Development Press
22 Amherst Rd.
Amherst, MA 01002

National Education Association
Distribution Center
West Haven, CT 06516

University Park Press
233 E. Redwood St.
Baltimore, MD 21202

Dear Reader:

Your feedback on this edition of **The Art of Helping** will help us produce a 5th Edition that better meets your needs. Please answer the questions below, tear this page out, fold where indicated, tape and mail. Thank you!

I am a: ☐ Professor   ☐ Inservice   ☐ Other_____
                     Trainer

       ☐ Student   ☐ Helper   _____

Types of clients and problems I, or my trainees, will work with:

How did you use **Helping IV**?

What would you like to see changed for the 5th Edition?

What would you like to see stay the same for the 5th Edition?

Any other comments you'd like to make?

BUSINESS REPLY MAIL

FIRST CLASS PERMIT NO. 24 AMHERST, MA

POSTAGE WILL BE PAID BY ADDRESSEE

**Human Resource Development Press
22 Amherst Rd.
Amherst, Massachusetts 01002**

- *(fold here)* -

Optional: Name _____
            Institution _____
            Address _____
            City _____ State _____ Zip _____
            Phone # (____) _____